Child Health Care

Living with children, working for children

Berry Mayall and Marie-Claude Foster

Heinemann Nursing

Heinemann Nursing
An imprint of Heinemann Professional Publishing Ltd
Halley Court, Jordan Hill, Oxford OX2 8EJ

OXFORD LONDON SINGAPORE NAIROBI
IBADAN KINGSTON

First published 1989

British Library Cataloguing in Publication Data
Mayall, Berry, *1936*–
    Child healthcare.
    1. Great Britain. Children. Health
    I. Title II. Foster, Marie – Claude
    613′.0432′0941

ISBN 0 433 00076 7

Typeset by Deltatype Ltd, Ellesmere Port
Printed and bound in Great Britain by
Billing & Sons Ltd, Worcester

613-04320941 62/   £9.95

Child Health WITHDRAWN

507 - 5245 .   RJ101

CONTENTS

FOREWORD

Health visitors have long suffered from what I have termed 'occupational paranoia': the conviction that health visiting (except by its practitioners) is little understood, greatly undervalued and therefore in danger of extinction in the not-too-distant future. Every new proposal for reform, whether of general nursing education, of the NHS itself, or of some aspect of its organization or structure, is seen as providing yet more evidence of health visiting's impending demise, and not without justification in some recent developments.

Yet the profession remains a formidable force for health promotion and the support of the public health, with no diminution in its vigour and vitality and an increasing willingness to face up to the challenges presented by the need for health visiting practice to change in some quite fundamental ways.

However, I wonder how much of the professional introspection and anxious debate about the future of health visiting in which we have taken part over the last decade or so might not be at least partly attributable to a deep (but not always fully recognized) discomfort at the conflict in perspectives and values around child health care generated by our work, and which this book examines. In reading the chapters which follow, therefore, health visitors – whether experienced practitioners, students, teachers or others closely involved in some way – will find plenty about which they may feel uncomfortable or even angry. Few will not identify with some of the statements made by the health visitors interviewed, as I myself have done, and perhaps feel defensive or guilty. The authors demonstrate a sophisticated and substantial insight into the health visiting experience and are highly supportive of the profession's attempts to operate within a complex set of often externally-imposed constraints and imperatives, but they nevertheless come to some compelling conclusions about why and how we must alter our perspective and practice if the concepts 'user participation' and 'partnership with parents' are to move out of our rhetoric and into health visiting reality. Berry Mayall and Marie-Claude Foster offer some rational explanations for the not always irrational fears we have for our future, giving us the chance to confront these and thereby to learn, and to change.

Their vision of health visiting as it could be, indeed *should* be, is wholly consistent with every positive development in health visiting currently being anticipated and promoted by the profession and its leaders and the book itself represents a very significant addition to the health visiting literature.

I commend its careful study to all with an interest in achieving a greater understanding of health visiting, and of its potential for further and more effective development within the preventive health services. But, above all, I commend this book to health visitors themselves who will find it rewarding at several levels: as an interesting and exemplary piece of research reporting; as a personal aide to greater 'user-friendliness'; and as a simply fascinating and highly readable account of health visiting at a time of challenge and change.

Shirley Goodwin
August 1989

PREFACE

The purpose of this book is to provoke discussion about child health care and the input of various people into this care: mothers, fathers, relatives, community nurses and doctors, day-care staff, social workers. We have used transcript interview data from a recent study to let some women speak for themselves about their views, their concerns, their work in child-care.

Keeping children healthy is an everyday affair, carried out by millions of parents – mostly female. These everyday activities are the practical evidence of a value-laden iceberg. Listening to parents talking about child-care is an education for the listener. It forces one to consider people's ideas about the goals of child-rearing and their visions (or constructions) of childhood, motherhood and fatherhood. For instance, when a mother says she wants her child to go to a nursery because it will help him become sociable, she is saying that sociability is a good thing in children. Then she goes on to say that she does not want him to be shy when he goes to school. Good social skills are important in the wider society. When a mother says she wants to go out to work, because it is up to her to provide good food, toys and books, she is arguing that it is part of her role as a mother to resource the household. So people's accounts of child-care, and of constraints and opportunities affecting it, tell us much about their goals for their children and about their models of, for instance, motherhood, fatherhood and 'the family'.

In the study we carried out recently, we listened to two main sets of people – mothers and health visitors – talking about child-care. Of course, since their work is different, their perspectives are rather different, and the comparison highlighted for us how unquestioning our own beliefs may be. We think it is interesting to describe these sets of beliefs so that readers may consider the implications of similarities and differences.

In Britain, so far as we know, mothers, with other women to help, always have brought up their children. This work mainly goes on in private and until comparatively recently it has not been the concern of the public domain. It's true that for at least three hundred years there have been people, mainly men, who have written books advising women how to do what they were already doing. But it is only in the last hundred years or so, that it has been seen as appropriate for us in Britain to pay – out of the public purse – for workers routinely and universally to advise and help mothers with child-care, and to do so by visiting their homes. Over the years then, health visitors have given generations of mothers support, offering both advice and practical help with child-care. The health visitor can be seen, and often is, as the friendly face of the health services, who is interested in the progress of normal children and will act as a referral agent on any problem the mother raises.

Like most societies, we in Britain have homed in on pregnancy and early childhood as a criticial period of life, and aim for universalist, on-going surveillance. There is no other age-group or at-risk group for whom we do this. We could for instance, institute health screening of the newly retired or of all middle-aged men (a group at risk of coronary heart disease). Once such a system becomes established its existence forces consideration of various, potentially difficult topics.

There are questions about the value of different people's views on child-care. Is there a generally agreed ranking order of different sets of people's views? For instance, are mothers' views widely valued as the best? Who thinks what on this issue? And whose views count when it comes to allocating resources? One of the things our study allows us to do is to consider how far workers in child-care, paid (nurses and doctors) and unpaid (mothers, other women, some fathers), think that the help and advice service is there to help mothers with *their* priorities, goals and problems, and how far do they think the service is there to steer mothers, children and possibly fathers in certain directions – towards certain lifestyles and goals, set by the paid workers (both field-workers and those who manage and employ them).

Surveillance, by its very existence, opens the door to the view that mothers do not know best, and do need help with child-rearing. We find in the literature by doctors and nurses a continuing concern with the inadequacies of mothers' knowledge (e.g. Royal College of General Practitioners, 1982; Freeman, 1983). This vision may obscure the commonsense view, and one held by some sociologists (e.g. Stacey, 1988), that people produce health themselves; and that mothers, in partnership with their children (and sometimes with their partners) work for their children's health and well-being. Input by paid health workers is relatively minor, though of course it can be very important, and even critical.

There are then further questions about welfare work with women. Is this work more like 'intervention' or more like 'partnership'? The word 'partnership' is commonly used in policy papers prepared by doctors and nurses. Both words are morally loaded. We choose to use the first and later discussions will clarify our reasons for this choice. So, how far do people, again the paid and the unpaid, think it is justified for outsiders, nurses, doctors, social workers and so on, to *intervene* in child-rearing? There is bound to be tension here between various considerations, and that tension may be fruitful and pro-ductive of checks and balances. At present in Britain there is much rhetoric about the importance of strengthening the family and encouraging it to function as an independent self-supporting unit: visions of each man (of course) as king of his self-sufficient castle! Yet there is also widespread and deep concern about child abuse and an increase in the time allotted by paid workers to monitoring child-care practices in families.

Such interventions suggest again a number of points. They suggest that we who pay think monitoring must be done and hope monitoring may protect the nation's children. In the last resort, we see the paid workers as advocates for the child, against the parents. In other words, the argument we as a society present to parents, is that they cannot be trusted to bring up their children well and to ask for help if they need it. An interesting issue that arose again and again in what mothers and health visitors said, was whether they were happy with the balance struck in practice between intervention and response. Thus mothers thought it acceptable that their practices be inspected, because they understood society's concern about child abuse, and were concerned themselves, but they also thought that, in general, it was up to them to seek advice and use services when they saw fit. They resented being told what to do. Some health visitors did not question their own right to intervene, both in respect of child-care standards and in respect of giving advice even when not asked for it. Indeed some health visitors felt they were responsible for ensuring the health and well-being of children on their caseloads. This feeling is a heavy burden; and, as we shall argue, it is both unrealistic and undesirable for them to take on such a responsibility.

At present it seems parents agree with welfare workers that they should monitor child-care practices; as representatives of the welfare state, they have a duty to protect children. Such interventions tread an uneasy tightrope between benevolence and control. Benevolence can be seen in the desire to protect children and to help parents rear them; but such monitoring and help can also be interpreted as measures that explicitly or implicitly aim to control women and their children. Some observers would argue in particular that welfare workers help to structure women's lives within the ideologies of the welfare state (e.g. Wilson, 1977; Orr, 1986). In both the short term and the long term, women are coaxed, encouraged or forced to conform to the model of dependent but caring women who hold 'the family' together.

So during our work we saw that an important theme emerging from what child-care workers, paid and unpaid, said concerned the extent to which they were and felt themselves to be powerful or powerless. Mothers bring up their children within a social framework that individually they cannot change. Social policies mould their lives; staying at home full-time is both the norm and the usual practice, and so they are dependent on others to bring in money to keep the family afloat. If, in order to resource the household, they want to do paid work, they are still dependent on society to provide day-care places, whether publicly or privately. Whatever they do, they lack power to shape their own lives and those of their children. Their daily lives are shaped by the repetitive tasks – providing food, washing, cleaning – that have to be done, and by the local physical environment: the housing, the streets, the shops. They also often find themselves cast as dependent, even childish, in their encounters with services. As many writers have documented, it is common for women, and especially mothers to be treated as not fully adult, and certainly not as independent people (e.g. Graham and Oakley, 1986). Yet within these contexts mothers may feel themselves to be in a position of some power, in their own homes, as managers, parents and to some extent as people. Women do act as house-keepers, allocating and managing the existing resources. Their day is not constrained by employers' time-tables and demands. They make many short-term and long-term decisions for and about their children. Some would say they have too much power over their children in the enclosed world of the nuclear family (c.f. Dally, 1982).

Health and welfare workers may also feel both powerless and powerful. At a day-to-day level, their work autonomy is limited by the demands of employers and by their working conditions. At a more general level, while they may recognize that social and economic factors determine or strongly affect people's health and health care, they feel unable effectively to influence these factors.

Yet doctors, nurses, social workers and others in welfare work have power over the people they are employed to serve. They, variously, influence the distribution of resources, pills, letters of referral, grants of money and access to housing. They have the power to label people, as having whooping cough or cancer, as good mothers, as social deviants, as uncooperative patients. These labels may affect people's perceptions of themselves, and the course of their lives. In health care work it has been observed that power relationships are firmly established and clearly to be seen and felt in operation by people in their encounters with health staff. An image of the family is reflected in doctor–nurse–patient relationships. The doctor–father, the nurse–mother and the patient–child play out their familial and familiar roles (*see* e.g. Oakley, 1986). The doctor is in charge of knowledge, diagnosis and resources; the nurse–mother takes orders and does the caring; and the patient–child is passive, managed and cared for. Most of us have experienced as patients being treated as passive and foolish and have felt our autonomy oozing away as we accepted the 'sick role'. As patients we sometimes feel we are treated like children.

But how if the target of the health care enterprise *is* a child? Certainly health visitors see themselves working *for* the child through the mother. They aim to change mothers' child-care goals and practices, often quite radically. Hence their feeling of frustration, if mothers resist, because they, the paid workers, lack the power to achieve their aims. Doctors in the preventive child health services, according to our data, are less ambitious and less frustrated. They recommend certain courses of action to mothers, but are happier with the idea that mothers will and should do as *they* think fit.

This book draws on interview data from mothers', fathers', health visitors' and clinical medical officers' perceptions of child health care. Many of the ideas that run through the book were stimulated and developed by the fact that these different groups talked differently about child-care. The fullest data are of mothers and health visitors talking and we have given long excerpts of their accounts to provoke discussion. We hope the book will be used by students and workers in health care work and in other 'person' work. Though parents are busiest of all as child-care workers, we hope some of them may find time to read this too.

The book starts with a chapter outlining the study and setting the scene, with a description of the areas where the study was undertaken. Chapter 2 considers ideas about child-care and childhood and

Chapter 3 considers ideas about mothering, motherhood and father-hood. These two chapters complement each other in that the two sets of ideas interlock and interact.

The next four chapters are about the various people's perceptions of the preventive child health services. Chapter 4 looks at child surveillance and health education, while Chapter 5 focuses on some of the tasks of health visitors, especially home visits and child health clinics. In Chapter 6, we consider the division of labour between paid and unpaid workers, and in Chapter 7 we discuss the implications of a multi-ethnic society and of focusing on individuals for health workers.

Finally, in Chapter 8, we draw out the themes that have run through the book and consider some broader issues. We make some general suggestions that may be of help for people planning services for children and their parents.

Each chapter has a similar shape. We start with parental perspect-ives because we think they are the standard against which to set the views of those who are employed to serve them. We draw mainly on mothers' accounts, but also on fathers' where appropriate. Then, on the same topics, we consider health visitors' views and, again where appropriate, those of clinical medical officers. Each chapter ends with a discussion, some suggested discussion topics and brief lists of books for further reading.

ACKNOWLEDGEMENTS

This book owes its existence to many people. We are grateful to staff in district health authorities who cooperated with us in our work, and to the people who willingly gave us time and thought during long interviews. We have received continuous support from colleagues at the Thomas Coram Research Unit and in particular, Charlie Owen.

We very much value the work of Shirley Goodwin, Roma Iskander, Ann Oakley and Sue Pike who read an early draft of the book for us.

We would especially like to thank Olwen Davies whose care and attention to detail saw us through several drafts of the chapters.

Finally we thank the ESRC which funded the two health care studies that stimulated us to write this book.

CHAPTER 1
CHILD HEALTH CARE STUDIES

This book is about the work of women in caring for children and in maintaining and promoting their health. It is about women who live in a particular country at a particular time, and whose work is affected at all points and at many levels by current social policies. Women care for 'the family'; and a whole battery of assumptions, laws and gaps in services ensure that they go on doing so, as Land (1978, 1983) documents.

While other countries have legislated to widen women's (and men's) choices of how to live as parents, and have provided services to back these policies, Britain has remained set in its patriarchal ways. To take some key examples: maternity leave provisions are among the most restricted in Europe, paternity leave provision, endorsed by every other EEC country, was recently vetoed by the British government and public day-care provision is virtually non-existent (Cohen, 1988).

We know from studies over many years that many mothers find the model proposed to them unacceptable and fight against it. Not all by a long way wish to stay at home full-time with their children. We know that poverty is particularly high among households with children because one income is not enough to support three or more people (Brown, 1988). We know that women's life-time earnings are seriously affected by the discontinuities most of them as mothers have in paid work (Joshi, 1987).

Women also know that there is a gap between rhetoric and reality: while increasingly public and political pronouncements emphasize the value of encouraging independence among citizens, the felt reality for women is decreasing choice and increasing dependence on their men and on such cut-back services as we have. While the advantages of 'community care' for the young, old and handicapped are emphasized in policy statements, women know that it usually means care within the *household* (not in the community) by women, unpaid and with almost no help *from* the community.

It is of particular concern that in Britain a rigid set of monocultural social values congenial to men are urged on a plural, multiethnic society where women are disadvantaged and those who are not white, indigenous and middle-class especially so.

People who provide services for women are also usually women: day-care, health care and welfare workers. As suggested in the Preface, these paid workers may also feel caught in sets of values and sets of social structures not of their making or choosing. During the course of our study of health visiting we began to understand the difficulties and tensions in their work in the context of the social structures and expectations within which they work. In some respects health visiting can be seen as an example which helps to throw light on women's paid work more generally.

Health visitors' work is valuable, but also stressful and conflicting. Some of the problems arise from chronic under-resourcing; female caring work has low priority for planners and policy-makers, compared, say, to male heroic surgery. Other problems arise from the tendency of caring women in our society to empathize with all the problems they meet in their work and from their inability to solve them. We are in no doubt, having 'lived with' the interviews for a year, that the caring work health visitors do is valuable and that the women cared for find it valuable. We do however think that there are ways in which health visiting could become a more satisfying and satisfactory job; and these we explore, and bring together in the last chapter.

PERSPECTIVES ON HEALTH CARE – TWO STUDIES

This book has arisen out of a programme of research work carried out at the Thomas Coram Research Unit (TCRU) London University. The central focus of this work has been people's ideas about caring for the health of young children and, during the course of this work, we have explored the perceptions of various sorts of people: mothers, fathers, health visitors and doctors.

The programme of work was initiated in the wake of the Black Report (1980), which amassed the evidence for inequalities in health and considered which groups are more equal than others. Overwhelmingly their evidence indicated social class differences in health status, in health care and in use of services. As they noted, of particular concern was the inequality in expectations of health at the time of birth and in the early years of life, though inequalities persist into later life too. The Black Committee considered possible explanations for the continuing differences, and its principal emphasis was on the debate between the argument that people's material circumstances and their position in the power structure largely determine their health status and their ability to care for their health; and the argument that individuals, whatever their circumstances, can make an important contribution to achieving good health.

In 1980 two of us at the Thomas Coram Research Unit (Berry Mayall and Chris Grossmith) carried out a study which considered the views of one important group of people in the community: mothers who care for the health of their small children. We set out to discover from them their ideas about what constitutes good child health care, what their practices were, and how easy or difficult it was for them to do what they thought best. We focused on mothers of children past babyhood – a much studied age (*see* Appendix 3). In order to study possible class differences on these points, we limited our sample in various ways, so that other factors were, so far as possible, cut out. So in our main sample we took only women who were white and were born in the UK, who lived in two-parent households, and who had a first child in the age-range 18–36 months. The mothers were all those who met these criteria and who lived in the area of one inner London District Health Authority (DHA) which was very mixed according to social class. We interviewed the 135 mothers once, at home, in depth.

We knew that like other researchers, we were omitting many important dimensions from our study. Most notable, we felt, was the omission of others of those who go to make up our multi-ethnic society. So we also interviewed in the same area, small samples of mothers who identified themselves as Bangladeshi, Greek Cypriot, and Afro-Caribbean or West Indian. The interviews were carried out by people from the same ethnic groups. This was a start towards carrying out work that took some account of ethnicity. As the Black Report noted, at the time there was little work that considered national or ethnic background as a factor in health status and health care.

This first study pointed to the conclusion that women's socio-economic position affects their health care. We found that they had a great deal in common as mothers, whatever their background. Their broad aims were much the same for their children, and their ideas about good practice were also similar, although women in higher social classes were more likely to hold some items of 'knowledge' or opinion also favoured by health workers (for instance that fluoride is good and sugar bad for teeth). But women's ability to care for their children seemed to them, and to us, to be seriously affected by their income, their housing, and the characteristics of the neighbourhood they lived in. Women in the higher social classes, who tended to have higher educational qualifications and the ability to earn good wages, were notably more successful than other women in finding satisfactory day-care, which in turn, enabled them to go out to work and thus provide a healthy standard of living for their children (Mayall, 1986). From our small samples of ethnic minority mothers, we could not draw firm conclusions, but we noted many instances where ethnic minority status seemed to put mothers at a particular disadvantage in their attempts to give good care, for instance, Afro-Caribbean mothers were especially likely to be allocated unsuitable housing for child-rearing. We also noted some particular problems faced by recent immigrants to the country, for instance, language differences reduced the possibility of health visitors giving advice (Mayall and Grossmith, 1984).

The experience of considering mothers' perspectives led on to a second study designed to explore some of the issues arising. It was clear that mothers have a lot of contact with preventive child health services in their children's early years. Though they feel responsible for their children's health and welfare and know how to care for them, they also seek information and help from nurses and doctors. It was therefore of interest to find out about the perspectives of health workers on child health care in order to see how far they matched those of mothers. In particular, health visitors seemed important to study, because, as accepted visitors to the home, as women and as a 'human face' in the NHS they seem to have considerable potential to help mothers. They might be especially useful to women who, for instance because they were new immigrants, lacked knowledge of services and of 'the system' in general – knowledge which mothers need to give good care.

We aimed to find a sample which would reflect the diverse population of mothers and households for whom health authorities provide preventive child health services. Such a sample would include rich and poor, those with professional work experience and those from poorly paid menial jobs; also people from a wide range of national and ethnic backgrounds. We used the same inner city area as before, because we knew it had this kind of mix. We decided not to pre-judge issues about who 'belongs' to which national or ethnic 'group'. So we chose, randomly, from all over the area, a sample where one-quarter were white and born in the UK and the other three-quarters did not meet at least one of these two criteria.

This was a small-scale, qualitative study, in which we aimed to get people to talk freely to us, on three occasions, and our sample was of 33 mothers. Each had a first child aged 21 months when we first talked with her. Twenty-four of them had a husband or partner living in the household and we managed to talk with half of these, too.

On the health worker side, we chose a sample of health visitors from all patches of the DHA who represented various kinds of workers: part-time and full-time, specialist and generic, clinic based and GP-attached, field-workers and seniors. Our stratified sample was 30 (three-quarters of all who worked for the DHA). Two refused, so we had 28 health visitors, and again, each was interviewed three times. In addition, we were able to interview (once) all the 11 clinical medical officers who worked regularly for the DHA. Most worked part-time; all were women.

In order to study whether health visitors' perspectives varied according to their working conditions, we also interviewed a sample of 20 health visitors, selected in the same way, in a county DHA. They represented one-quarter of all the health visitors working for that DHA. So we had in all 28 London health visitors and 20 County health visitors.

This is a very brief summary of the samples and how we obtained them. Those who want a more detailed account of the design and methods will find it in Appendix 1. The study was carried out by the authors of this book.

The 33 households

We set out here some information about the households studied. The points we have chosen to focus on are those which seemed to parents and to us to be important in affecting how satisfactorily they, as households, lived, and in particular how easy and difficult it was to care for the child or children.

Perhaps the first point to make is that there was a multitude of nationalities in our sample. Apart from British-born people, mothers and fathers between them came from 20 countries, and from most

Table 1.1 Sample households

Mother's country of origin	Years in UK	Household	Paid work	Housing (floor)	Money problems
UK		MFX	F	Flat (2)	
Middle East	2	MFX	F	Flat (6)	
Africa	7	MFXA, relatives	F student	Flat (4)	
UK		MFX	M,F	House/ garden	
UK/WI		MX, relatives	Relatives	Room (3)	✔
Africa	3	MFX	M F student	Flat (0)	✔
UK		MFX	F	Flat (1)	
Europe (F UK)	15	MFX	M,F	Mais (0)	
UK (F Europe)		MFX	F	Flat (1)	✔
UK/Cypriot		MFX, relatives	M	House/ garden	✔
Far East	2	MFX, relatives	M,F	Room (2)	✔
UK/WI		MX	M (at home)	Flat (2)	
UK (F Australia)		MFX	M	Flat (1)	✔
WI	20	MX	M	Flat (0)	✔
WI	19	MX, relatives	—	Flat (3)	✔
India	3	MFX	—	Room (0)	
UK		MFX, lodgers	MF lodgers	House/ garden	
UK/India		MFXA, relatives	F M at home	Room (0)	
UK		MFXA	F	Flat (2)	
UK/WI		MX, relatives	Relatives	Council house/ garden	✔
India	3	MFX	—	Flat (1)	✔
WI	10	MX, relatives	—	Flat (6)	
Africa	4	MFX	F	Flat (2)	
UK/WI		MX	M	Flat (3)	✔
UK		MFX	M,F	House/ garden	
Far East	8	MFX	M,F	Flat (0)	
S Africa	2	MFX	M	Flat (0)	
Europe	5	MFX	—	Flat (1)	✔
Indian sc	3	MFXA, relatives	F	Flat (4)	
UK/WI		MX	—	Flat (0)	

Europe (F UK)	9	MFX	F	Flat (2)	
India (F Europe)	15	MFX	F	Flat (2)	✔
Africa	7	MX	M student	Flat (2)	✔

Father's country of origin is given if different from mother's.
Indian sc = Indian subcontinent.
MFXA = mother, father, focus child and baby
WI = West Indies

parts of the world (see Table 1.1). For 14 mothers and 10 fathers, a language other than English was their first language, though in only four cases did we interview parents in another language. While some parents, especially the mothers, had been in Britain for only a few years, virtually all these sets of parents felt they were here to stay. The sample included nine women who had been here for up to 5 years, five for up to 10 years, five for over 15 years. Fourteen had been born here and these included six whose own parents were born abroad and who saw themselves to some extent as West Indian or Black British (four mothers), Greek Cypriot (one) and Punjabi (one).

An important factor perceived by mothers as affecting their lives and those of their children was the number of adults around and available. It was important to mothers to have people to talk with about child-care; this continuous detailed child-focused conversation was a principal source of their increasing knowledge. So it is of interest to note here household composition and whom mothers mainly relied on for child-care talk. Sixteen of the households conformed in composition to standard British models: they had a father and mother and child (our focus child of 21 months) and some a second, younger child. Another eight households had father, mother and children plus others, mostly grandparents or sibs and their partners. Five mothers lived just with their children and four lived with their children and their own parent(s).

Most women thought of their own female relatives as the principal people to talk with about child-care and to offer practical help: their mothers, mothers-in-law and sisters. Not surprisingly therefore those who had been in this country for a relatively short time – up to 10 years – felt badly off in this respect. For all but one of them, their parents and parents-in-law were abroad and they missed them badly. For many, ringing their relatives abroad was an important item to be regularly budgeted for.

Another set of points needs to be made here, to do with material standards of living. We knew from other work that having spacious accommodation, including a garden, matters to mothers for many reasons but especially because they perceive children need space to play and play safely. Parents everywhere prefer houses with gardens to flats off the ground! They also aim to own their property: as regards their children, one important reason is so they can adapt it to keep their children safe and happy, an option which is not open to council tenants. In this sample of households (Table 1.2) only four owned a house and garden; all these had been here all their lives and three were dual-career households. Another 'professional' class household owned their flat and garden. One (joint) household lived in a whole house and garden as council tenants. Most of the rest were in council flats without gardens, incuding 14 who lived on the second floor or above. Finally, three households lived in one room, again with no access to a garden.

Table 1.2 Type of housing

		Council Hous. Ass.			Room
Own house/flat + garden	Council house + garden	Ground	1st	2nd or above	(large household in council house)
5	1	5	5	14	3
					n = 33

An important driving force among many of the women, as well as of the men, was to earn money to improve the household's standard of living. Though of course people's motives for doing paid work are many and complex and certainly include the short-term goals of keeping the household afloat, it was striking how powerful was the urge to earn and to learn in order to better themselves. Thirteen of the mothers did paid work 'now' and a further 12 urgently wanted to. But finding day-care and finding paid work were two linked problems, especially for newcomers.

Thus a high proportion of these mothers of young children wanted to do paid work. Table 1.3 shows that only 10 households conformed to UK norms where a father is out in paid work and the mother is at home full-time with the children. In 15 households mothers worked or were students. In eight households, household income depended on relatives and social security benefits.

Finally, it seems appropriate to note here the kinds of work mothers and fathers did. It was an unsurprising finding of the earlier study that

Table 1.3 Paid work, including students

Type of households	F	M	F+M	No parental work	n
(M + F + children + others)	10	3	8	3	24
M (+ others)		4		5	9
n	10	7	8	8	33

indigenous households with mothers and fathers in professional work now or in the past were more successful in reaching a satisfactory way of life for themselves and their children and, in particular, these mothers were better resourced to give good health care. In this study we considered whether parents felt they were living as they wanted to, in relation to the type of paid work they did and the number of years they had lived in the UK.

There are difficulties about using women's work as any kind of marker. Girls who do well at school may not go on to further education or training. Many women do not do paid work that fits with their educational or training level. Access problems, social expectations and child-care work affect these transitions, careers and relationships. Immigrant and ethnic minority women may be especially unable to obtain qualifications: and to be unable to do paid work; or they may do work that is below their abilities, training or previous work. So for women there are no simple relationships that hold good on ability and qualification levels; and on education and type of work.

With all these provisos, we give in Table 1.4 the present or most recent paid work of the mothers, in these categories: professional work requiring extensive study and qualifications beyond school

Table 1.4 Mother's present (past) paid work, including students by years in UK

Years in UK	Professional	Office	Domestic	None	n
Up to 5	1 (2)	0	1 (2)	3	9
6–10	2*	0 (1)	1	1	5
15+	1	1 (1)	0	2	5
UK/EM	1	1 (1)	2	1	6
UK	4	0 (1)	0 (3)	0	8
n	9 (2)	2 (4)	4 (5)	7	33

* Both these mothers were students, and one also worked weekends as an agency nurse. UK/EM means born in the UK with ethnic minority status.

level; office work requiring training; and various kinds of domestic and service work. Seven of the mothers had no paid work experience.

Perhaps two points stand out in this Table: the relatively high rate of current paid work among those with 'professional' experience, provided they had been in the UK for a long period; and the low rate of current paid work among those relatively newly settled in the UK, whatever their past work experience. We will return to these topics later, in connection with the usage of and demand for day-care for children.

Fathers had been longer in the UK than their partners, in almost all cases. They were mostly in paid work, but a fifth were not (Table 1.5). For fathers, there is no clear relationship between years in the UK and paid work. The reason for this seems clear. Finding adequate day-care in the UK demands expertise in 'the system'; how to work it against all the odds to find a day-care place. Newly arrived mothers did not possess this expertise. But fathers' work is not affected by fatherhood and by the absence of day-care provision, and most of these fathers, like those in every study, saw themselves, rather, as financially responsible for the household, as the main breadwinner.

Table 1.5 Fathers' present (past) paid work by their years in the UK

Father's years in UK	*I,II*	*IIIN*	*IIIM*	*IV,V*	*No information*	*n*
		Type of paid work (RG classification)				
Up to 5	2(1)			1		4
6–18	1	(2)	0	4		7
UK born	4	0	2(1)	2		9
No information	1	0	1(1)	0	1	4
n	9	2	5	7	1	24

Resourcing the household and providing an adequate standard of living was a major source of concern for many of the parents in our sample, referred to several times during their accounts (Table 1.6). Of the 14 households where parents seemed particularly worried, six were one-parent households where the mother either had no paid work (3) or was low paid (3). Of the eight two-parent households, two had both parents not in paid work and in five cases one parent worked; in one household both parents worked. So while unemployment was a severe financial problem for five households, low paid work was so for nine.

People's perceptions of how desperate is their need for more money

Table 1.6 Perceived money problems by family circumstances

| Money problems | 1-parent household | | 2-parent household | | |
	No paid work	Paid work	No paid work	Paid work	n
Emphasized	3	3	2	6	14
Not emphasized	2	1	1	15	19
n		9		24	33

to provide an adequate standard of living will depend on many factors. While it seemed to us that some of the more newly immigrant households were desperately badly off, according to parents' perceptions it was not particularly those who had had only a short time to make their way here who felt poor. Notably, proportionately more lone mothers than mothers in two-parent households felt poor. As they said, they had moved down from a reasonable income for one person to no paid work or little to finance two people. Absolute need, comparison with what others have, with what one had before and thinks reasonable or desirable, will all affect perceptions.

This brief description of the households in our study has considered length of residence in the UK, some pointers to satisfaction with social support, housing, paid work and perceptions of poverty. The description has made a start in showing how complex our sample is! There are few patterns that emerge strongly; but white professional two-parent households were very well placed to provide a healthy life for selves and children – in terms of housing, good support, satisfaction with paid work and day-care, good income. They also reported satisfaction about how they and their children led their lives.

By contrast, a group that stood out as finding it especially difficult to provide a good life for adults and children were those who had been in the UK for only a few years. Migration had disrupted their lives in many respects; and working towards a good life here was difficult, as they faced a complex and unresponsive 'system' and some hostility from the 'host' community.

The health visitors

We give here some details about the backgrounds of the two samples of health visitors we interviewed. The points we have chosen to set out here are those we thought, at the outset, might be important factors, helping to account for group differences. As it turned out, some did and some did not! We note these differences in the course of the book.

The 28 London health visitors were mostly born in the UK and four were Black British. Over one-third of them had experience of living and/or working in societies other than the UK. As well as nursing qualifications, half had 'A' levels and a few had higher qualifications. Half of them had one or more children of their own. Most of them had moved quickly out of hospital work, after their basic training, and 20 of them had had over 5 years experience in health visiting work, mainly in London. Table 1.7 sets out some data on the two samples.

Table 1.7 London and County health visitors compared

Age in years	*20+*	*30+*	*40+*	*50+*	*n*
London	6	11	7	4	28
County	2	5	11	2	20

Academic qualifications		*'O'*	*'A'*	*Higher*	*n*
London		10	15	3	28
County		17	3	0	20

Years as hospital nurse (after qualifying)					
		<5	*5*	*10+*	*n*
London		20	5	3	28
County		14	6	0	20

Years as health visitor					
	<5	*5*	*10*	*15*	*n*
London	8	12	5	3	28
County	7	5	3	5	20

Has own children		*Yes*	*No*		*n*
London		14	14		28
County		13	7		20

Living and/or working experience in other societies					
		Yes	*No*		*n*
London		11	17		28
County		4	16		20

The 20 County health visitors were mainly white, indigenous women. Only two came from other societies and few (four) had experience of either living or working in other societies. They were an older group than the London health visitors and more had children of their own. Few had academic qualifications beyond 'O' level. Like the

London health visitors, most had left hospital nursing early on. For most of them their work as a health visitor had been in county areas, rather than in cities.

Later in the book (Chapter 5), we describe the health visitors' satisfaction with working conditions: such as the type of attachment, the staffing, accommodation, back-up services. We also consider their perspectives on issues such as the control over their work by management and superiors and how far they felt able to do the job they wanted to do.

Clinical medical officers

The 11 clinical medical officers (CMOs) interviewed were all those who worked on a regular basis for the London DHA. They were all women and most had children. Most were white, UK-born, but three came from the Indian subcontinent. Almost all had qualified as doctors over 10 years ago. Some had taken up clinical medical work in the preventive child health services partly because it fitted better with motherhood than other doctoring work; half worked part-time and half full-time. Most of them had been in this type of work for less than 3 years, and while four felt committed to it, most planned to move on to or to combine CMO work with general practice.

Until a few months before the interview, the CMOs had been employed as peripatetic workers, but DHA management had then reorganized their work so that they were attached mainly to one clinic and were also responsible for giving a medical service to nurseries and schools in the same patch. This was perceived by the CMOs as a much better arrangement. It allowed staff at the clinic to develop team-working and facilitated doctors' continuity of contacts with children and parents.

The London area and the County area

We give here a brief general description of the areas within which we undertook the study: the inner London one where parents lived and London health visitors and clinical medical officers worked; and the county area where the comparison sample of health visitors worked. The data come from local and national statistics.

The London DHA is co-terminous with a local authority borough.

It measures about 2 miles wide by 5–6 miles long. It is densely populated and has many busy roads, some quieter neighbourhoods, and some small parks, with larger open spaces on its boundary. The area includes some affluent areas where high housing prices reflect demand from wealthy people. Apart from these relative newcomers, there is also a population of people who have lived in the area for several generations, either in their own or in council property. In all, over half the households in the district live in council property, and there is also some private renting.

Council property ranges from run-down pre-war estates, to small modern estates of houses and maisonettes. The owner-occupied housing is mostly in Victorian terraced houses, some divided into flats.

The population of the area is multi-ethnic and socially mixed. One-quarter of 'heads of household' were born abroad, and there are also many ethnic minority people born in the UK. About one-fifth of 'heads of household' are at the top of the social class scale (RG I) and the same proportion at the bottom (RG IV and V), according to local statistics which use the Registrar General's classification.

By national standards, the area has high provision of day-care places (Table 1.8): day-nursery places for 10% of children under-5, and child-minder places for 6%. For 3 and 4 years olds, nursery school and class provision is also high with 64% of these children having a place. As is often the case, where public provision is high, voluntary provision is low: playgroup places are available for 30% of 3 and 4 years olds. There are no figures available for mother and toddler groups.

The county DHA area is more difficult to describe because its boundaries cut across local authority boundaries, and some data are

Table 1.8 Day-care and education places for under-5s

Area	% of ≤5s having places		% of 3 and 4 year olds having places	
	Day nursery	Registered minder	Nursery school/class	Playgroup
London	10	6	64	30
County	1	6	25	62
UK	1	4	23	32

UK figures source: Cohen, 1988; Tables 5.1, 5.9, 5.12
Note: in all cases these are approximate percentages derived from data for 1985.

not available for the DHA itself. However, the area is very different from the London one and can be broadly described. It is much larger – about 20 by 15 miles and it comprises one large, industrial town and some smaller ones, with villages and rural districts. It is within commuting distance of London. It is an affluent area by national standards, with small pockets of deprivation, centred mainly in parts of the big town. Most households own their property and most people live in houses rather than flats. Council properties tend to be concentrated in small estates. Compared to the London area, twice as many heads of household do work classified by the Registrar General as I and II (43%), and less than half are in classes IV and V (9%). Few people are from ethnic minorities, with the largest concentration, again, being in the large town.

The area has low provision of day-care places by comparison with the London area (*see* Table 1.8), and in this respect is more similar to the national picture. Thus, there is a day-nursery place for only one under-5 in a hundred; there are places for 6% of children at registered minders, but none of these are sponsored by the local authority. Only a quarter of 3 and 4 year olds have a place at a nursery school or class, but playgroup provision to some extent compensates for this: 62% of children go to them.

The interviews and the data

We elicited people's views on child health care through semi-structured interviews. That is, we had a list of topics to be introduced by a question, and a set of prompts to use if necessary. We followed where the interviewee led, in that we encouraged development of points raised and also altered the order of the topics if the interviewee led the conversation in certain directions. We also had in front of us and firmly in our minds a list of the questions we as researchers were aiming to answer and we tried to cover all these during the course of the three interviews. Since the two of us shared the interviewing, it was important to have a systematic structure of this kind, as well as a flexible approach.

As regards how to interpret these people's accounts we have assumed some principles. We take it that what they said does bear a close relationship to their views and that it is therefore valuable to try to describe what they said. We also think it is part of our job to consider these views against the social and economic contexts of people's lives. So we describe what people said, quote it and interpret it. The quotations are often long – and we think thought-provoking, and we hope they *will* provoke discussion and comparison. Rather than offer discussion of the quotations ourselves we have often left it to the reader.

Most of the detailed findings considered come from the study of parent and professional perspectives outlined here. In addition, we refer constantly to the earlier study out of which this one grew: the study of two-parent household indigenous mothers' views. This is available as a book: *Keeping Children Healthy* (Mayall, 1986). There are a few other studies we can draw on for comparison. These we refer to a good deal, and for easy reference we have given a brief description of them in Appendix 3.

CHAPTER 2
CHILD-CARE AND CHILDHOOD

In this chapter we shall explore some aspects of how mothers and health visitors think about the care of small children. We shall consider the items each group sees as important, and the areas they think are problematic. The chapter aims to raise discussion about people's knowledge about child-care, about the nature of children and about the role of professionals in advising mothers about the care of children.

The history of child-care is a history of changing fashions, based on widely varying ideas about the nature of children, the goals of child-rearing and the most effective methods of reaching those goals. Even that sentence makes an assumption that children should be reared, rather than just cared for.

In the last 60 years alone, child-care 'experts' have promoted a number of widely varying views on the nature of children and suggested a huge range of behaviours for parents (but they usually mean mothers) to engage in. These 'experts' do not always make their own assumptions explicit, and the reader has to read between the lines to understand them. Christina Hardyment's book on these changing fashions, and Sandra Scarr and Judy Dunn's succinct account of a range of psychologists' approaches, are excellent (and easy) reading for exploring 'expert' assumptions and for making one re-think one's own assumptions. For it is important for anyone working with and for parents of small children to think hard about the 'facts' of good child-care. Are some practices better than others? By which criteria? How far is the child-care advice offered to parents moral advice, based on ideas about the perceived goals of child-rearing? Let us start by comparing how two groups of people, mothers and health visitors, approach child-care.

APPROACHES TO CHILD-CARE: MOTHERS AND HEALTH VISITORS

What kind of approaches and what kinds of knowledge do mothers and health visitors bring to child-care? Our study led us to think there are broad differences between the two groups of people. Here is a brief outline of some major points.

Bases of knowledge

Essentially, mothers' knowledge is experiential. It is based on knowledge of the individual child and of others in the family: the child's character, history, the way her mind works, her likes and dislikes. It is knowledge that develops and deepens as the child grows, in response to the child's behaviour and development. Health visitors' knowledge is book knowledge. They learn what 'experts', notably psychologists, say about how children develop.

Other sources of knowledge

Both mothers and health visitors also acquire knowledge from child-care books, health education leaflets, and TV programmes. (All the mothers, except two, and most health visitors had child-care books.) Mothers learn from other mothers – and some health visitors mentioned doing so too. Mothers value the detailed continual conversations about children and child-care they have with their own mothers and sisters, and with friends who have children. Mothers also explicitly continue with traditional ways of behaving or take into account the value of so doing. Both mothers and health visitors may have knowledge gained from bringing up children. In addition, health visitors learn from experience, on the job, of what works in child care. They may go on specialist courses (for instance on sleep problems) and they learn from talking with colleagues.

Context of knowledge

Mothers' ideas about how to care for the child will take into account the needs and wishes of other important people – relatives and friends both in and beyond the household; and of the constraints and opportunities in which these people operate. The health visitor may seek to acquire insight into this complex of considerations, to the extent that she sees herself as a family visitor (and can find the time and opportunity).

Success in child-care

For mothers, success in child-care is judged on at least three criteria: first the child's happiness now, and the happiness of other important people. Second, whether the child is doing as well as other children they know. These two criteria may be less important for health visitors, who may rate success more in terms of the long-term goals they see as important: that is, child-care is good if it includes behaviours which some theorists say will lead to such outcomes as emotional health in adulthood and to achievement in schools and in adult paid work. Third, mothers, and health visitors too, judge parental care according to whether the child attains developmental targets as set out in standard tests devised by psychologists and medical 'experts'. Health visitors and to some extent mothers ascribe praise or blame to the mother according to how well the child 'performs' on these tests.

SO ARE THERE ANY FACTS OUT THERE?

A very striking feature of these two groups' approaches to child-care is the status or quality they give to their knowledge.

As we noted above, mothers' experience of living with their children provides them with one source of knowledge about which practices work and are good. When they are faced with a new circumstance, a decision or a problem they will seek views or advice from many sources. In our study we discussed with mothers who were the people whose views and advice on child-care they valued and trusted. All 33 (except one) had at least one valued person to turn to (as well as, in some cases, the child's father). But it was striking that mothers who had been in the UK for less than 10 years felt the lack of their mothers and sisters; migration had cut them off from these valuable sources of discussion and advice.

Some mothers (13) valued advice *only* from relatives and friends;

notably their own mothers, mothers-in-law, sisters, and friends with young children. So for over one-third, health workers were not in the top rank as people to turn to. However, most (19) knew at least one health worker whose views they trusted, and five mothers said they would turn only to health workers. Mothers also sought opinions from books and leaflets. They were fully aware that there was a range of views 'around'; that knowledge changes and that they were right to do what seemed best, all things considered. So what they knew was a mixture of family traditions, adaptation to the needs of the child and advice from many sources, including that of health workers, in most cases.

Health visitors were strikingly different. Most made it clear to us that they saw themselves as having *factual* knowledge. Other words they commonly used to describe their knowledge were: objective, detached, correct. And some explicitly made a link between being a professional and having a body of correct knowledge. Few took the view that knowledge in child-care is largely a matter of opinion and that other people's knowledge might have equal value with theirs (Table 2.1). The majority indeed assigned the same factual quality to their views on diet, developmental stages, the value of stimulation, the value of children eating with the family, the importance of establishing certain habits and so on. (Quotations later in this chapter and in Chapter 4 give examples.)

Table 2.1 Health visitors' perspectives on their child-care knowledge

| | Health visitors | |
	London	County
Their view is correct	20	16
Some discussion of plurality	3	0
Acceptance of plurality	5	4
n	28	20

The big exception to this rule was the topic of immunization. This is a controversial topic which has received detailed and careful thought by health staff. Health visitors talked in careful detail about it. They explained to us that there were various opinions about contraindications (re measles and whooping cough),that they did their best to keep up with changing views and that they discussed the range of views with parents. This relativistic approach was in strong contrast with the firmness with which they told us that, say, 'eating with the family' was good and that they tried to educate mothers to promote it.

These broad contrasts in the two groups' perspectives are interesting especially in view of the health visitors' perceived role as health educator. This topic is discussed in detail in Chapter 4. Here it is important to note some points arising out of these contrasts.

First, we live in a very varied society in the sense that people bring to the care of their children a huge range of beliefs influenced by their own history and the contexts within which they live. Notably, we live in a multi-ethnic society with great differences according to socio-economic status and background and people's knowledge of child-care is correspondingly varied. In a nutshell, there may be many good ways of caring for children, and many acceptable goals of child-care.

So it is valuable for those who work for the health and welfare of other people's children to consider the status of their own knowledge, and the value-bases on which much of it rests, before offering it to parents. Perhaps it is also valuable for such workers to consider making their values explicit in any intervention.

Finally on this, if it is the case that much knowledge in the field of child-care is opinion, and value-based at that, then people who work on behalf of children need to consider, if they aim to educate, which educational goals and methods to adopt. Do they aim to extend parents' knowledge about varieties of child-care practice, or to teach them to think about the goals of child-rearing, or to train them in behaving in certain ways? And, in each case, how would they justify these aims? Which methods are then appropriate? Should they go for a top-down approach, or, at the other extreme, a discussion between people whose views have equal value?

The next section of this chapter considers mothers' and health visitors' perspectives on child-care, focusing on their views about the child.

MOTHERS' PERSPECTIVES ON CHILD-CARE

We described in Chapter 1 some important factors that made life for mothers with children easy or difficult; household income, housing, the neighbourhood, the availability of adequate day-care, frequent contacts with other mothers. It is in respect of these aspects of their circumstances that many women see problems and seek change. Warm spacious housing, child-friends, safe streets, enough money to provide for the household; these are important contributions to the child's well-being and health. As mothers they value having other mothers around to help them gain in knowledge and confidence about child-care. It follows that when mothers talk about caring for their children they stress these powerful influences on their own and their children's lives.

Like health visitors they talk about the importance of diet, sleep and exercise as contributing to good child health. They also stress hygiene, keeping children warm and dental care as contributors (fewer health visitors stress these). The delightful, challenging and rewarding parts of child-care are: responding to the child and helping her as she grapples with the acquisition of skills, especially speech; helping her take a part in family social life; watching her enjoy and make increasingly important contributions to relationships with people in the household and beyond.

Here are some, typical, things that mothers say about their 21 month olds:

'She's one of those people who knows what she wants. If she wants to write, she wants to write, and if you can give her a pen, OK. And if she wants you to read something, you've got to read, you know. She knows exactly what she wants.'

'Her vocabulary has changed a great deal, it has improved, much wider now. She says a lot of words. And she copies everything you do. You have to be so careful of what you do and what you say. She may not say it the same day, but a few days later you hear her come out with it. You've got to be very careful, because she watches every movement and she's a proper copy cat.'

(Yesterday) 'She was in a mood to go out. I mean like now. She always gets her trousers on and things, ready to go out.' (She gets her hat on?) (Child is standing there with her outdoor clothes). 'Oh yes, she demands it. She takes me to her wardrobe. I've got to take her out.' (Does she help you with dressing nowadays?) 'Oh yes, she does. She takes out what she wants. Like now – she takes out her trousers. She's waiting for me to dress her ready to go out.'

(Yesterday) 'I plugged the television on and I said to her to switch it on. I watched tele and then I said to her, "Switch it over to the other channel", you know. She gets annoyed if I go and switch over to the channel – she goes and switches it back and tells me off (laughs). And – I can talk to her about anything really. And cuddle her and give her a kiss.'

'Ah well (before he was born), I was unhappy because I was all alone.

My husband was out working and I was all alone. Now he's my companion. And before I found nothing to do. Now all day long, the day is filled.'

'It gives a lot of happiness, watching a child grow. You just know a bit about how you grow yourself . . . She changed – 6 months ago you had to do most things for her, you had to feed her, you had . . . now she handles the spoon herself, she walks. If you go out, she says "Bye". If you say to her "Shut up" she says "shut up". You play music – she dances and she says "Bravo" and claps.'

'Oh, when he starts laughing and comes in (to bed, in the morning) and go on you and kissing you and giving you a hug, when you get up in the mornings. He starts smiling all right (laughs) and when you smile back at him, he just roll over and come over you, kissing you.'

'She's a lot more forward, a lot more forward than she ever was.' (So she's learned to do new things?) 'She sometimes helps me to tidy up – she tries to put things in the washing machine. She always did that – she tried to tidy up, but she used to throw it in the dustbin. Now she is not so keen on the dustbin, now she actually looks at me first. She's very proud of what she does in her potty . . . She is trying very hard to form sentences, very very hard. She's not frightened of anything or anybody. She's a forthright little girl and if she does not like something, she will tell you about it. She talks to people on buses and everywhere and we've got to a stage where we've got to be careful what we say in front of her, because she will repeat it . . . She's got very good eyesight and very good hearing, but she's stubborn. Sometimes she hears you, but she will deliberately switch off. I must admit *I* do that sometimes. And she's also quite good at, if she sees an advert on television, she can actually sing what goes on. Beforehand she would be looking at it, but . . . and she's been watching programmes now especially with children and she can laugh at funny things that happen. She is just very different now.'

'She plays with toys now. Bricks, building things. Then (6 months ago) she didn't play – it was just physical learning, walking round the table, learning to walk. Toys as such weren't as interesting. Now, she's very keen on books; her little wooden animals, her soft toys. They've been around, but she's started to play with them. Dolls. She play-acts. She gives them tea. Imaginative play. She's playing more. She responds to instruction better. I can have much more constructive talk with her. If I want to distract her, she can do a lot more things. We do singing, she likes singing games, looking at books. There are more laughs.'

'Now she is like a little person to me, instead of when they are babies, you don't class them as being anybody – they are just a baby, feeding, put them to bed, change them. Now we can talk to one another, you know, it's like, it's nice actually, it's company.' (What sort of things do you enjoy?) 'It's hard to say, it's just nice, you know, it's hard to remember, the things they do are nice and make you laugh . . . are quite funny.' (Is it easier or more difficult now, looking after her?) 'I think it is much easier once they are walking and start to talk a lot more, it is much easier to look after them. Also if you go out you can just go in somewhere and have something to eat together you don't have to take all the baby foods and I used to find you could not go anywhere because you would worry about all the things you need to take with you.'

'It's an incredible pace of learning. He's learned to mimic, you know, he copies everything you do and if you find yourself scratching your nose you'll suddenly see him scratching his nose. So you've now you've got to be quite careful what you do. His speech is – his vocabulary has widened incredibly and he's now stringing words together. You know, he doesn't just say bird or mama, he'll say "here it is". You know, he puts a few simple words together. He's learned, he's got this, like the big Lego, 6 months ago he couldn't fit them together, now he can fit them together and take them off and put them back together. Things like dressing, he tries, he pulls things off, he loves to do that. Now I get his jumper off except for one arm and he pulls it off and he feels very pleased with himself. He tries to put his shoes and socks on. He tries to put his mittens on. He's learning a little bit about himself as well, because when he – I've only just noticed this in the last few days – when he wants to urinate he starts to hold himself and he goes "oh". But he's learning a bit about his own body, now as well. I'm sure there's lots more that I can't think of.'

These quotations from what mothers say point to a number of themes that are common to all or most of these mothers.

We were struck by the fact that mothers perceive their child as a *complete person*. As they look back over the first year and a half of the child's life, they stress the child's achievements in moving from what she was at birth to her being now. The child is seen as having a clearly defined personality, a set of characteristics: she may be obstinate, persistent, ingenious, carefree, a bit of a worrier, sensitive, not afraid of anyone or anything, cautious, a bully, and so on. Children of this age have become *affectionate*, they initiate cuddles and kisses with the people close to them; that makes them rewarding and delightful, and also encourages the mother to think of the child as active in developing relationships. So children of this age have become people to interact with, they are company, they are fun, amusing, they contribute to their mother's enjoyment of life through a two-way relationship.

Another important common theme is that mothers perceive their children as *active* in the sphere of learning and of social life. They demand to extend their knowledge; they insist on responses to their questions, and to their initiations, they take their mothers (and fathers) to their coats, in order to encourage outings; they drag them towards books and balls, they insist on playing with adults. They are keen to take on jobs, about the house: they commandeer dust-pans, dust the television, stir the cake-mix, wash up. They take responsibility for tasks that directly concern them (tooth-brushing is commonly cited) and insist on doing it their way; they struggle to dress themselves, are feeding themselves, some are taking an interest in controlling excretion.

Very noticeable in all this were two points: the child as *independent operator* and the child as *communicator*. Drawing on their year and a half of motherhood, these mothers emphasized the child's drive towards autonomy: her attempts to take control over certain jobs, to make her own decisions about how the day was to be spent, how much sleep she wanted and took, what sort of food was to be eaten when, what sorts and numbers of outings were desired and should be promoted. Some ($n = 12$) laid particular stress on the fact, noted with approval, that the child was now much less dependent on her parents, was able to function on her own, and played happily on her own, or with other children, for longer periods, without constant reference to her parents.

This view of the child as an independent actor, naturally keen to learn from people and the environment, putting energy and hard work into acquiring skills, is somewhat different from the child as perceived by the health visitor, as we shall see later.

The second point that emerged strongly from the mothers' views is that by 21 months the child has become an *effective communicator*. Even much younger children use gestures and language (however imperfectly by adult standards) to interact in complex ways with people around them. But for mothers the acquisition of clearer speech marked a major breakthrough in terms of the adults' relationships with the child and the child's ability to manipulate her world. *All* the mothers stressed the child's linguistic competence and development and most saw this as resulting from the child's enthusiasm for learning as well as from the adult's role in talking with the child.

Why was speech so important for these mothers? At least three strands can be found in the mothers' remarks. First, of course, the child could now communicate her wishes and needs, so she was easier to care for. The distressing situation known to all parents, where the child clearly wants something but you cannot fathom what it is, now occurred much less often. Secondly, there was now more of a two-way relationship: the child was now a person to be communicated with through language; she was fun, company, and the parents could gain some insight into the child's way of thinking. Thirdly, language acquisition was seen by mothers as important because it marked an important achievement. This view no doubt partly reflects the fact that they have internalized the messages of the media, the schools and the professionals – that speech acquisition is critical for the child's success, and that parents have a role and duty to bring on the child's speech. But it is also an important change because it means, in practice, that the child has now become a part of human society who contributes to social relations and is not merely a 'becoming', to be helped through stages towards person-hood.

What mothers say about their children strongly indicates that they have confidence the child is doing well and will go on doing so. Their emphasis is on what the child achieves, in the context of relationships and a physical environment which allow her to learn.

HEALTH VISITORS' PERSPECTIVES

Health visitors' views read very differently. In the first place, health visitors emphasize childhood as preparatory to adulthood. They see children as going through a series of developmental stages. They have to be helped through those stages by their mothers. Childhood is thus seen as essentially preparation for adulthood. Each stage has problems attached to it. Notably for instance, 2 year olds are refuseniks, asserting their will. This is not to say that mothers do not see children as going through stages. It is to point to the fact that many health visitors put particular emphasis on the problems attached to those stages (at least half the health visitors talk in these terms); the need to warn mothers about them; and the preparatory nature of childhood.

> *HV:* 'This is the time (21 months) when mothers start wondering. "Is my child progressing as he ought to?" "Is he doing all the right things?" "Now why isn't he talking as well as the one next door?" And this is the time when they throw tantrums and try to be firm about what they want or don't want and parents start thinking, "Oh well, he is naughty" when he's actually not naughty. This is the time when they become demanding because they don't like their parents talking or paying attention to other children, therefore they are more demanding on the parents. This is the time that's worrying the mothers because they start climbing up and down the stairs and mothers are almost having heart

attacks thinking he's going to fall headlong or whatever. And she worries if she has not got a gate. This is the time they're going in and out of things and she worries if she has not got a fireguard. And this is the time she worries in case he pulls the saucepan or the kettle and she has not got a cooker guard. And she worries in case she is downstairs he comes out of his bed and comes downstairs or whatever. Or this is the time he wants to experiment so mother is always having to be on the go and be very alert because this is the age of the terrible twos.'

I (interviewer): 'Do you see it as your job to help with that?'

HV: 'Well you can point out the dangers, you can point out how best they can cope, but try to reassure them to make them more relaxed to be aware of the situation so that they're not constantly tensed and worried, in a state of panic.'

I:'What do you think brings about good health in a young child?'

HV: 'I think a very contented mother and father, really a good household, where the mother is aware, is not over anxious, about the health. But you find where there's a mother who is taking everything in her stride, that child thrives very very well. But as soon as there are some problems in that house you can see it through the child, then the problems start to happen, I think specially, I should think, things like sleeping problems and also crying baby all the time, you know, generally things like that.'

I: 'With a child of that age (21 months) are there some health care practices which you think are important for keeping the child healthy?'

HV: 'Well, things like diet needs at that age, and socialization really you know with other children of that age, and also you know, generally keeping the child happy and contented and you know, clean and keep an eye on things for the child, and stimulating the child more or less really, because all toddlers at that age go through various stages, they go through – negative to positive, they are more negative at that stage anyway, and it really is sort of trying to advise parents how to deal with that negative stage, and then all that the toddler is doing is not really naughtiness, it's just trying to reassure them, so that the parents can say "oh well you can operate".'

I: 'Do you introduce this topic with parents?'

HV: 'Oh yes.'

I: 'Why?'

HV: 'I introduce it because this is the sort of thing that all kids go through, at one stage or the other, but it's best if the parents are aware, really, say for example, if the mother has just got a first child and she hasn't got a clue about what is going to happen, so it's my duty really to forewarn her of the various stages that the child will go through, and to say, "it's all right, it's nothing abnormal", because parents do compare their children with each other's, friends, neighbours and relatives, and to say "look your child is your child, and that child is unique!, and you can't compare", though they still do. But at least they will be reassured

that yes, the child is doing well and it's just a phase and that there will
be the next phase, so it does give them reassurance, I like to warn them
about it.'

We may note the health visitor's view that it is her job to warn the
mothers in order to reassure them. But, three questions here: Do all
children go through these problematic stages? Should health visitors
promote that view? Will it reassure mothers?

A second important feature of health visitors' accounts is their
perception that children's long-term emotional health and especially
their emotional health in adulthood is directly dependent on the care
they receive now. The child is likely to be irreparably damaged if she
does not make and maintain a secure attachment to one caregiver who
is with her virtually all the time. This is a point we will return to in the
next chapter, but it's important to refer to it here, because it seems to
form the framework for the health visitors' view on the importance of
certain behaviours by mothers with their pre-schoolers. The first of
these concerns stimulation, and the second discipline.

I: 'So what do you think brings about good health?'
HV: 'It's obviously coming from a happy, healthy home, to begin with.
That gives them a great start, providing they haven't had any handicaps
to overcome.'

I: 'What do you mean by "healthy"?'
HV: 'Well-nourished, kept reasonably clean, stimulated, talked to and
loved. Routine as well, as I think routine is a very important thing in a
child's life. I think it's one of the big security-givers. I think a child who
has a reasonably strict routine, who knows where he is, has a lot of
security and they know what's happening. For instance, if they go to
bed more or less at the same time, and have meals at the same time. I
think they can carry little differences as well when it comes to holidays
etc. in their stride then, when they look forward to coming home again
and settling back in the routine again. I see that happening with my
own children. I think really much depends on the parents, and the
peace and harmony within the home. When the mother goes through a
bad patch, the baby goes through a bad patch, the baby then often has
destructive behaviour and you get these other psychosomatic things
and it's very inter-related.'

Stimulation is a current buzz word among people who advise
parents about their children. The idea is that purposeful programmes
of talk, often with play objects as a trigger, will bring on children's
speech. In the absence of such purposeful programmes the child will

be 'under-stimulated' and will not 'reach its full potential'. All the health visitors talked about this purposeful stimulation as one of the major tasks of children's main care-givers. Now, as we noted earlier, mothers think children's speech develops through the ordinary give-and-take of household conversation which adults and children both enjoy and initiate, and through the child demanding to learn. If anything, mothers have to dampen down their child's exuberance for learning in the interests of their own survival. Who hasn't said to their child, 'Leave me in peace for a minute – stop asking questions!' In this connection an interesting recent study is one that analysed children's conversations with their mothers and found the ordinary home an adequate linguistic environment and a richer one than the nursery school (Tizard and Hughes, 1984).

I: 'So you think play and stimulation – you said that's your "big subject". Why do you introduce that subject?'

HV: 'Because I think each parent owes it to their children, you know the child, to encourage their true potential, to realize it, and one of the best ways is – sooner or later – sooner at 5, they have to join the education system and that is very important for the child to be seen to be doing what the child of that particular age should be doing. And I start off from the word go with this, from the very first time I have contact with the family, like usually about 12 days, I talk then, it's a continuous theme throughout my contact with people.'

I: 'Do you think sometimes parents need help with this?'

HV: 'Yes. You see I take it right from a 12-day-old baby where I go and I say to the mother you know, talk to your baby, a lot of eye contact, the most important thing, forget about expensive toys, the most important toy is your face, and take it through over the 6-month baby, exposure to books, I take it all the way along.'

I: 'Do you think it's difficult for some parents to give their children adequate stimulation and play?'

HV: 'I do. In this area in particular, I'm thinking of the majority of the clients who meet in each other's homes and groups and things, and the children are there incidentally, they talk around their children, but it's not much meaningful.'

I: 'Why don't they do it?'

HV: 'Sometimes for the simple reason that no one has ever told them that they could relate to their children in a different way. Maybe because they feel they have a social need to be with other adults and exchange adult ideas or just have adult type discussions, and the children are there, they can keep an eye on them, they're happy, they're playing around, this input doesn't have to be constant. I don't know . . .'

This health visitor returns to the theme later when discussing ways in which parents differ from her in views on good child-care.

'I find in this area . . . most of the parents are very young and the extended family is very much in evidence around here. So when it comes to things like play and stimulation we differ, greatly. Because I'm all for the early introduction of books and suitable play-material, you know – to hell with the status element of the type of toys you buy for your child – just sensible toys that children could learn from. And they're all for the status ones, the expensive . . . the expensive bikes, and whatever . . . and I'm saying, "Look, well you can use the Toy Library", "You can go to the library and get books; you needn't buy expensive books for your child". "There are lots of books in the library. You should read to your child; you should talk to your child." Not just, she's there – he or she is there and I'm talking at them. You know, just make time for them and talk to your children . . . that's very difficult. It's a great struggle, because they – the young parents' idea is to go around to tea, we all have tea together, all the children run around quite happily, and no-one actually has a meaningful exchange with a child and . . . it's . . . I find the acquisition of speech in this area very slow when you compare it to other areas. And in fact I recently have had to revise my thinking and accept that that child perhaps is not slow – speech development is not slow – it's quite appropriate for the society in which that child finds itself.'

Childhood is preparation in many important ways for health visitors and most (three-quarters of both samples) stressed the importance of moulding the child to fit in with family and societal norms. It was important to train the child into good habits so that family life could run smoothly, for instance, to establish regular sleeping times which fitted (to some extent) with those of the parents would make life easier for both adults and children. The health visitor's job was to encourage mothers to manage the child *now* so that later on appropriate habits would be established.

I: 'Are there some health care practices which are important, which you think are important, for keeping the child healthy? And why?'
HV: 'Yes, I think it is important at that age that they should have a routine, not a very rigid routine, but some sort of routine so that the child knows what is likely to happen in the order – so that meals are reasonably you know, at set times, and I think that at that age quite a lot of distraction comes into keeping a child happy and exerting some structure to their day and discipline if you like really, because they can be really quite wilful and disobedient at that age and I think usually children that are over-indulged are usually quite miserable because

they don't – instead of having firm boundaries that they can work against, they are so busy testing the water all the time they really don't – you know, they get themselves all muddled up.'
I: Do you raise this topic with parents?'
HV: 'Sorry do I?'
I: 'Do you raise this topic with parents?'
HV: 'Yes, we do talk. We talk about some sort of flexible routine from quite early on – I don't believe in for instance cuddling babies to sleep in your arms or letting them fall asleep on the couch. When I first came up here we had a great spate of people with 18 months to 3 years olds with sleeping problems and when we actually did a little bit of investigation they were always the children that had never ever been put in their cots – they had always been cuddled to sleep right from babyhood and it was tremendously difficult for the parents to break the habit and these children were waking up at night, then they needed to be cuddled to sleep again, they never got themselves into a routine for themselves, so we talk about this right from the beginning antenatally – I don't know how much goes in antenatally, but then we can build on it later.'

The following account from a mother illustrates the point that not all parents view 'sleep problems' from the same perspective as health visitors.

(She is talking about her encounters with her health visitor.) 'I've never been worried about X's sleeping even when he was sleeping badly and I think (the health visitor) she's trying to be helpful in that I don't have any problems – I don't think I have any problems and she wants to try and help me so she'll always ask me about X's sleeping and I say "Oh, it's fine". And she'll say "How do you get him to sleep?", and I say, "Well, I put him in our bed and he falls asleep and then he goes in his cot". And she'll say, "Well you know you might be causing trouble, you might be better to put him in his cot straight away", and I say, "Well, it suits us, we're all very happy".'

We should note here that people's ideas about what families are and how they should live, are moral ideas. They are about concepts of the good life. So for instance, in reply to a broad question, 'Do you think food is important at this age? What practices do you think are important?', many health visitors answered not only, or even not at all, in terms of diet, but in terms of family meals. Children should sit down 'with the family' to eat.

'I think that the child has to be given the opportunity to participate with the rest of the family in their eating patterns. Obviously when the father is not at home it can be difficult. And even if that child does not stick to, for example sitting down with the mother and the siblings for breakfast that pattern should really try to be encouraged as much as it can, so the child becomes used to a time of the day when he or she is expected to eat and I think that this is one principle which should be encouraged with a child of that age. If he chooses not to eat at that time then I would encourage the mother not to become anxious about that and then just go to the next time when it would be appropriate for the child to eat.'

The reasons health visitors gave for 'eating with the family' were various: it encouraged children to eat enough; it encouraged them to eat what the mother had prepared for other people (so it was less trouble for her); and very importantly, it encouraged family cohesiveness. (Fathers were seen to be a problem, because they were not often there in the child's day!) As the next health visitor argues, eating with the family could also provide children in later life with a strength to withstand disintegrating pressures on the family coming from outside.

'I think it's very important – food, not for the physical well-being of the child but the social aspects of it. I think it's extremely important that families do sit down for meals together, it's something that some families don't do. I think children eat better with the family around because it's a time – as the child get older there's school and adolescence and it is a good habit to have, to keep the family together. I do really think that the family is very important. I think meal times are very often the only time sometimes as children get older that they can be together, so I think that food is important for two ways, for the health of the child and the social aspect of it.'

Toddlers needed habits, training and routines not only to make them suitable for family life, but also so that they would be fit to join the wider world. Mothers got children ready for mother and toddler groups, these prepared children for playgroups, playgroups for nursery school and finally the child would arrive at primary school as a confident, capable child.

I: 'If we take another topic now, contacts with other children, the same set of questions, how important do you think contacts with other children of this age group are?'
HV: 'Yes, I think that is important – I mean they don't play with other children in that age group, but I think it's important that they mix with other children, and don't have entirely an adult situation to live in, but when they do you know, or only with adults, when they then get to a

bit older, 3, and the playgroup looms, the children can't relate to other children. And you have a lot of problems with mums leaving them, so I think that really they need to mix with other children all the time.'

However, behind these ideas about fitting children for family and wider social life, are other ideas about relationships between children and their parents. The child's will – seen to be emerging around 2 years – was a problem not just in practical ways, but because it offered a challenge to parental authority. The child must learn who is boss.

(Health visitor has been talking about a particular family.)
I: 'You've talked about good points in the parents' care of their child. Are there any bad points in their care?'
HV: (Longish pause) 'I think very little. They tend to be a little overprotective. I . . . that's not . . . it's not taken to extremes. The child is occasionally allowed to dominate the mother because the child is a very clever toddler and will refuse food by going into the fridge (laughs) and point and get everything the child wants. I don't see that as a problem because I think . . . the fact is, it's a two-parent family, and the mother is getting flashes of insight into how she's being manipulated! I don't see a lot of bad care, really.'

This next health visitor sees meal-times as good because they encourage children to eat enough and to eat meals rather than snacks and because they provide a setting where mothers can establish who is in charge.

I: 'What do you think are good practices on food for this age-group?'
HV: 'I think it's very important that they actually sit down for meals and that they are not fed on the run, the mother following them around with a spoon. Because so many children are difficult at this age, so many, practically all of them at some stage are, so I do think that it's important that you sit down and sometimes that involves putting them into a high chair so that they can't move, but they are at the table with the parents because they don't want to sit still at this age, life is too busy for them to be bothered, and I point this out to the mothers that they are just so interested in everything else and rushing around from one thing, to another, that to sit down for a meal is really quite boring, especially if they are not very hungry.
I: 'Do you think some parents need help on nutrition for their children?'
HV: 'Well I think some people need reminding, there's an awful lot of bad nutrition around. Most people do know what constitutes a healthy diet, that fruit is more important than crisps and sweets and things. I think they need it spelt out for them at times that they don't have to give way to them. A 21 month old who's demanding sweets and crisps I

think it's the beginning of the discipline angle at that age, they are beginning to try on who is stronger and the mother has got to be stronger – it is bound up with food and the mother does need to have control and say no.'

It is worth pausing here to note that the clinical medical officers took a somewhat more relaxed view of child-care and child development than health visitors did. Several went out of their way to say they thought mothers did a good job of child-rearing and that bringing up children was not a problem, on the whole. However nearly half also thought some mothers were worriers and that the doctors' role was to give information and, an important function of the doctor, to reassure mothers that the child was normal and the child-care adequate.

It seems likely that their orientation to their work, and their work experience may account for this stance. The clinical medical officers did not see it as part of their job to seek out mothers. Their job was to check children brought by mothers, essentially for defects, and to respond to mothers' questions and worries. Theirs was a responsive rather than an interventionist stance. And they kept at a distance from the details of people's lives. Further, their experience of monitoring large numbers of children and of accepting the principle that there is a large range within which children can be deemed normal, may well lead them to the view that most children do well enough and that most children, in Winnicott's famous phrase, get 'good enough mothering'.

SUMMARY AND DISCUSSION

We have suggested that mothers' approaches to and knowledge of child-care differ in some important respects from that of health visitors. Mothers' knowledge is based on direct, continuing experience and includes consideration of a complex of interpersonal and socioeconomic factors. While health visitors may recognize the value of this perspective, their own is heavily influenced by psychological theories about child development. Notably, the emphasis mothers give to the child as an active enthusiastic learner and as a valued person contrasts with health visitors' view of the child as an incomplete person to be moulded, taught and managed in the interests of long-term goals.

It is worth suggesting here that what we have learned about mothers' and health visitors' perspectives on childhood and child-care suggests reasons why mothers, after the first few months, turn less often to health visitors for advice. Their knowledge and confidence has grown and they value direct, experiential knowledge and discussion; in addition their perspectives diverge from those of health visitors.

It is particularly interesting that the two groups regard so differently two important aspects of child growth: the integration of the child into social life and the child's learning of skills and speech. Mothers regard these as taking place in the ordinary give-and-take of family life, providing the household is reasonably housed, and has enough money and caregivers. Health visitors tend to regard these as problematic areas of child development, where all depends on the adults' input. Discipline, moulding the child into certain habit patterns, stimulation are viewed as areas where mothers may fail –from ignorance or from poor motivation.

To summarize the health visitors' perspective in a word, their approach to child-care seems to be problem-oriented. Developmental stages have problems attached; moulding the child is a problem; and getting mothers to understand the tasks of childcare and to carry them out is problematic.

Why do health visitors think personal, behavioural problems are so prevalent? Explanations may lie in their training and working conditions. Health visitors in training study both sociology and some child development theory. Sociology may help them understand some aspects of the social contexts within which parents rear their children, but if parents, and health visitors, see difficulties arising from poor housing, household poverty, adverse characteristics of the neighbourhood, and lack of day-care, the health visitor has little power to help. On the other hand, her training in child development leads her to perceive a role for her in informing and teaching certain parental behaviours. She feels able to intervene at the personal, individual level, though not at the wider societal or resource level.

Furthermore, her work is supposed to be universalistic. That is, she is supposed to visit everyone with an under-5, and inevitably she will try to find a role for herself in every household. A few of the health visitors in our samples said that there were households where child-care was adequate and the parents had no social or individual problems for which health visitor intervention was appropriate. But most health visitors thought they had an educational role in all households, because child-care could always be better, and parents must always strive harder to enable the child to reach its full potential (*see* for instance HV on page 29).

Perhaps, too, health visitors face a difficulty, again arising from their training, in distinguishing between relatively factual matters in child-care, and opinions, theories and assumptions. For instance, it may be relatively well established that certain feeding practices lead to good physical health in a child. But there are few child-care practices where one could demonstrate cause and effect. Further, once you get beyond physical outcomes to emotional or psychological outcomes you are obliged to consider the goals of child-care, that is, what kind of adult do you aim to develop through certain child-care practices. For instance, one might aim for a highly individualistic, aggressive, competitive entrepreneur, or for a group-orientated, cooperative sort of person.

In addition, like everyone else, health visitors make many assumptions about how people should live. For instance, many thought there should be an established pattern of events in the child's day, and the caregiver's day. Many health visitors thought that fostering close family relationships was a good thing. (We may note that in some recent child sex abuse cases some 'authorities' have argued that where a father was hurting his children, the professionals' aim should be, at almost all costs, to keep the family together.) Most endorsed the value of the full-time caregiver (usually the mother) and the bread-winning other (father). Obviously we all make assumptions about what constitutes the good life. But where people see themselves as health educators or monitors of parenting, they must face the difficult task of facing their own assumptions and of devising appropriate practices.

DISCUSSION TOPICS

1 What child-care practices do you consider to be good and why are they good?
2 How can health workers reconcile their own values with those of parents?

FURTHER READING

Hardyment, C. (1984). *Dream Babies. Child Care from Locke to Spock.* Oxford: Oxford University Press. An exhilarating account of 'experts' ' pronouncements on child care – over the centuries.

Hoyles, M. (Ed.) (1980). *Changing Childhood*. London: Writers and Readers Publishing Cooperative. A varied collection of poems, stories and articles about childhood. Highly recommended.

Scarr, S. and Dunn, J. (1987). *Mother Care/Other Care*. Harmondsworth, Middx: Penguin. Good summaries of the changing views of psychologists on child development (especially in Part two). This book is also good reading on dilemmas of modern motherhood – to be or not to be a 'working' mother.

Tizard, B. and Hughes, M. (1984). *Young Children Learning*. London: Fontana. An enjoyable and fascinating account of 4-year-old children's conversations with their mothers. It challenges the view that teachers do better than mothers in talking with children.

CHAPTER 3
MOTHERS, FATHERS AND OTHERS

In this chapter we look at parental and health worker perspectives on adults as carers of children. Perhaps two major and linked themes emerge from the interviews with mothers, fathers and health workers. The first concerns parents' use of time and the second children's relationships with adults and children.

There is only a finite amount of time for people to carry out the tasks or activities of parents. These comprise essentially: earning money to finance housing, food, clothing and so on for the household; and caring for the child. Some may also say that to remain healthy in our society adults need to engage in the public world of work; if they cannot do this their health may suffer and so may their care-giving to the child.

The second important theme concerns the child's relationship with other people. Issues raised included, notably: whether the child needs a continuous 24-hour care by one adult; the role of fathers; what, if any, is the value of children spending time with other adults and with children.

We noted in Chapter 1 that 24 of the households were 'nuclear' (mother + father + child/ren) and in eight of these there were also friends or relatives in the households. Nine mothers were 'lone', but four of them lived with their parents. The allocation of child-care varied. Thus in nine of the 'nuclear households' fathers (according to both fathers and mothers) played a large share in child-care, including four cases where the parents agreed care-time and responsibility was split fairly evenly. Where the fathers, or partners, were not resident, they did not, according to the mother help much. Among the 'lone' mothers, only three, who lived alone with the child, seemed to be solely in charge. The rest shared the care, to a varying extent, with their relatives.

The assumptions we make about mothers as the main care-givers were variously challenged by some households. For instance, in one household, the father was the main care-giver during the day, both agreed on this, while the mother was in paid work. It was especially interesting that he talked in the way we are used to hearing mothers (but not fathers) talk: in very great detail about the child's character, her feelings, her progress, her needs and her wishes and about how his life was affected in every way and at every point by his daily and continual responsibility for the child. In another household, the mother claimed that she was one among several more or less equal care-givers: whoever was there cared for the child, and he went to whomever he chose, which varied according to his mood, his need and his perception of what each care-giver could and would give him. In a third example, in one household the main care-giver was the child's grandmother – a fact that was graphically emphasized when, in the middle of the interview, both women being present, the biological mother suddenly left the room to cook a meal, leaving her mother to go on with the interview.

On this matter of who gives the care, the exact breakdown may be difficult or impossible to sort out, but the important point is that our sample points to variation in our multi-ethnic society. At least two thoughts are provoked by this variation. First, children in many households do make important relationships with more than one (or two) adults. And second, people wishing to affect child-care will need to take account of diversity in household type and in the division of labour in child-care.

MOTHERS' PERSPECTIVES

In the first chapter we explained that of our 33 mothers, 13 were in paid work, two were students and many others wanted to work. Thirteen children regularly spent some time with other care-givers (mostly at minders, a few with relatives or at nurseries) and another 12 mothers wanted a day-care place 'now' for their child.

So a high proportion of the mothers did paid work. Mothers, like other adults, work for a variety of reasons. Notably they need money to finance a household with dependants. They work to preserve their identity, to share in adult company, to pursue interests and careers. In our society to be in paid work is considered a desirable, even normal, feature of adult life.

However, as is well known, it is difficult in Britain for mothers to combine paid work with child-care. Jobs and pay are structured so that you have to work long hours to earn a living wage. There is no policy orientation towards the provision of adequate day-care services (in quantity or quality) to enable mothers to work. The net effect is that where a mother aims to do the two main jobs of a parent: providing financially and providing good care (by herself or by others) she is almost bound to be engaged in a stressful enterprise. In our sample, many could not find day-care (12) or they wanted a better place (3). And while only one mother out of 13 wanted to give up paid work altogether (hers was a physically exhausting job), seven would have preferred shorter hours, so that they could spend more time with their child.

It is striking that only 10 sample households conformed in behaviour to the normal family beloved of policy-makers and politicians: father in paid work, mother at home full-time with the children. It is especially striking that of the 10 mothers, the only four to express unmixed satisfaction with this way of life were the four white indigenous working-class women. They said they had no ambitions to go out to work and were happy at home. As Steedman (1982) suggests, in her riveting analysis of 8-year-old girls' stories, working class girls in Britain are early socialized into acceptance of the wife and mother role. In general, mothers felt themselves to be living under serious difficulties; their lives and those of their children were severely constrained by problems and frustrations in these two areas of paid work and day-care.

The third major problem was housing. Most (27 of 33) were very unhappy with their housing, in particular because they saw it as bad for their children's health and welfare. The commonest drawbacks were that it offered insufficient playspace indoors and out, and was cold and/or damp. One mother makes many, common, points.

M (mother): '(The neighbours) started saying about our kids jumping up and down screaming and making a lot of noise, so after that, I thought we'll try and be a bit quiet, because it might be that we were making noise for them, but since the council (F complained to the council about neighbours' noise!) they've been pretty good, I mean you know – it's been – I've been restricted since that, for doing things, which I don't really want, because I mean he's growing, he wants to run, jump, play, so you know, now I thought well I can't restrict him, I mean he's only a child, he doesn't know any better and he wants to do these things, he's got to do these things to grow. So that's one point about the building and also it hasn't got a garden, there's nowhere for them to play, like it's all right now, but when he gets older he'll want to play out and everything, so I'll just have to get him to parks and things. But hopefully I mean in another few years we might be able to afford a house. I just hope so.'

I: 'Are there any good points about your housing?'

M: 'The good point about this flat is that it's big, so there's a lot of room, although there is no space to play downstairs, or anything, or a garden, it is a big flat, so they've got the opportunity to play you know. I mean my friend's got a flat and it's very tiny, and you can't play, you can't run about, I mean if you've got three or four kids in here playing, there's room, they run up and down the hall, he can ride his bike down the hall, whatever, and the kitchen and my other sitting room is very big as well. So that is one opportunity. The other thing about it is – a bad point – is that it's got no central heating, so in the winter it's very cold. Because of that we had to put a fire in the other sitting room, the sitting room-cum-kitchen sort of room, we had to put a fire down there and in the winter we have to have a radiator in the bedroom, because it gets very cold with it being such a big flat. I think they're thinking of putting central heating – the tenants' association they are pushing for central heating and double glazing, but whether we get it or not is another thing. Otherwise it's a pretty good flat. I mean we were lucky because we had to leave – where we were living before it was with my parents-in-law, and they owned it, and they were selling it, so we had to really move and I was pregnant at the time, so we were lucky to get this, this is our first offer and because we had no choice we had to accept it, without central heating. Although I really did want central heating with a young baby, but luckily enough he was born in the summer so it gave him time to acclimatise really. Get used to it – I mean instead of just being born into the freezing. So it wasn't so bad.'

Housing, paid work and day-care were seen as interlocked problems. Children who lived in poor housing were particularly in need of the space and comfort of good nurseries: mothers could achieve better housing only by earning the money; they couldn't earn the money because there was inadequate day-care.

It is noteworthy that many of these women were trying to make their way against such difficulties in a country relatively new to them; and that in 12 cases there was no other adult bringing in a regular income (either they were lone mothers, or any other adult was unemployed). Women who were managing to make a relatively easy passage through the rough seas of parenting an under-5 in Britain were the well-to-do, indigenous mothers, who could *buy* their way out of the situation: they bought nannies and private nursery places.

By contrast, mothers recently arrived in this country lacked knowledge to work the 'system'. This mother is a trained teacher who

has lived in Britain for less than 3 years:

I: 'Have you had any contact with the clinic lately?'

M: 'Yes I went to ask about Peter, because he gets frustrated, he screams. I don't know what to do with him, for him. I don't know what he wants. The HV wasn't very helpful – she didn't make any suggestions. It's because he can't speak – he understands, but he can't say what he wants. He gets frustrated. He gets very aggressive, crying. It's terrible. I start crying because I don't know what he wants. I get a book and show him. I play with him. Sometimes I take him to a friend's house – there's a little boy there. Then he's better. Or to the creche. He spends – he can go 9.30 to 1.00 and 2–5. You can leave him there. But he doesn't spend all that time. Just a few hours.'

(By the time of the next interview this mother had moved house to another borough. Here there were no children in the block of flats and the health clinic could only suggest toddler groups, which were a long way off. The mother went to these, but found they were unfriendly. She desperately wanted to get back to work. Or to go on a course to learn more, or to train for work here.)

M: 'I asked the clinic for a centre (a college). They gave me an address. I went there but they haven't much courses – for me. They had yoga and . . .'

I: 'They gave you an address at the clinic?'

M: 'Yes, and I went there. It's very close to here, in one of the churches, and I've been there but they haven't much variety. And just this mother and toddler group. And there is no creche available with all the courses. So I can't go.'

I: 'What about the clinic – are there groups there?'

M: 'No.'

I: 'They have a list of groups?'

M: 'Yes and I went to some of them. It's very good for him. He played very happily. But for me no. Because people aren't very friendly. I don't know why. There was a lady there – she sat beside me all the time and I asked her some questions – she answered me and I saw her next time and she looked as if she didn't know me.'

I: 'Who did you see when you went to the clinic?'

M: 'The HV and the doctor. And I talked to both of them. And they gave me these addresses. I said I've got a problem and they said, mother and toddler group. They weren't much help. Because he's playing the same there as he's playing here. I hope they can take him for nursery. That would be fine. Peter would change. Because it would be full-time. He would be full-time with other children. And he can learn from them. At the mother and toddler he saw me sitting and all the time he came and said Mummy give me that thing, take this thing. And they are just 2 hours. It didn't seem much help for me. And from yesterday I told my husband I decided not to go. Because it's again much more difficult for me. Because I sit with people – they talk nothing. There was two ladies there, they talk to each other. The lady who runs the creche – she's busy with the children, and she gave them drinks, you know. And she gave them toys and she's talking to them all the time. And we are sitting alone. I told my husband. I feel more free (if I'm not there) – I can do something. I think I'll take him once or twice a week, not every day.'

It is also worth pointing to a similar set of contrasts, based solely on social class, found in an earlier study (Mayall, 1986). There all the mothers were white, indigenous and living with their husband or boyfriend; but it was the well-to-do ('higher' classes) who had adequate housing and day-care, and where the mothers went out to work. Households where fathers did unskilled or semi-skilled work had poor housing, the children were not in day-care and the mothers were at home as full-time child-carers.

The reader will have noted that little so far has been said about fathers' role in providing for the household. If the father was acting as bread-winner, surely there was no problem? But many parents did not see the income from one adult as sufficient to provide for three people (or four if there was a second child). And indeed the evidence is that in Britain households with children are more likely to live in poverty than other households (Brown, 1988). In any case, as aforesaid, there are many reasons why mothers wish to work.

However, it should be said that the fathers in our sample tended to see the division of labour as between mother and father from a traditional perspective. Of the 12 interviewed, eight claimed that in theory and in practice, the father's main role was in providing for the family; and they saw the mother as the principal care-giver in terms of time given to child-care and in terms of responsibility for the child's health and welfare. Since most of the 12 fathers not interviewed were unavailable (at least partly) because of their long hours of work we may perhaps infer that most of them held similar views. This point is supported by other studies, for instance by a recent (Australian) study of fathers. Of those in 'traditional' households, 59% thought being the breadwinner an important role (Russell, 1983). Only four fathers (in households where parents worked equal hours) claimed that mothers and fathers shared tasks and responsibilities equally. Mothers tended to agree with the father's assessment.

It is also important to note that this chapter has started with a discussion about paid work, day-care and housing not in order to clear 'background variables' out of the way or to dispose of a side issue in child-care. Not at all! Mothers saw adequate household income, adult well-being and a satisfactory social and physical environment for the child as central contributors to her health and welfare.

Also central were the main relationships in the child's and the parents' life. Like health visitors, mothers thought loving, secure relationships between the child and its parents were crucial to the promotion of the child's health. Indeed that relationship was seen as central to a woman's identity once she gave birth. But, as suggested earlier, most mothers saw themselves as people who were mothers. They wished to spend a lot of time with their children, because both adult and child needed and enjoyed each other's company. But few wanted to be with their children all the time. Only four of the 33 fitted, in this respect, the advertisers' and policy-makers' image of the perfect mother.

We said that 25 of the 33 mothers either had day-care places for their child (13) or wanted a place (12). This was a topic mothers raised themselves, in many cases as an overwhelming concern. We ourselves did not ask them to talk about day-care – nurseries, minders, playgroups and so on – although in the third interview we did ask them whether they thought socializing with other children was important for their child's health. But most mothers raised the topic spontaneously. The need for day-care arose from two main interpretations of household members' needs: first, as before, many mothers needed to work; second, they thought their child (21 months) benefitted from being with others. The most common argument they gave (18 mothers) was that it was important for children to learn to be part of a group, in order to learn to share with and respect other children and in order to help them develop as sociable people.

> *I*: 'Do you think mixing with other children is important for her health?'
> *M*: 'Yes. She's still on the shy side, but she's improved dramatically since she's been going to the childminder. I think I said this last time. And she's now much more willing to, other children are not a threat to her anymore, you know. She's used to other children and how they behave. She is interested in that. Now, if we go along to a pub or something and there are other children, you know, she is holding on to us, but she's also catching their eye. You know she's willing to go out as well as holding on. So I think it's, I think she's OK now, whereas we were a bit worried about it before. She's still shy though – she does take time to relate.'

Many observed that their children enjoyed being with others and were noticeably alert and absorbed (11) and some (6) saw it as necessary to the child's well-being. Children who had no company but that of their mother became frustrated and bored. In addition, children were seen as learning skills, notably language from each other (7).

> *I*: 'Do you feel you and X are living your lives the way you want to?'
> *M*: 'Yes, I'm happy with it, but I still feel he should be with other children. Once I get out to work I don't want him to be at home with his grandmother. He should be out with other children. Even now he needs to be with other children, 'cos when other children come round he's a different person. He gets really excited. You can see the difference in him. This is why I try and take him out and be with other children as much as possible. If we know anyone that's at home that's got a child we go round there. He needs to be with other children.'
> *I*: 'Are there advantages of him being with children?'
> *M*: 'Yes, his speech develops, potty training's easier.'
> *I*: 'He copies?'
> *M*: 'Yes, he copies from the other children. When it's just him he'll play me up. And he'll have set meal-times and he'll wear himself out! And go to bed a bit earlier! There is a difference with him – you can see it.'

Eight mothers thought that learning to be independent from their mothers was important for children; to learn that they could be happy spending time away from their parents. Finally, on this, 12 mothers thought that it was valuable for children to get on with and feel happy with more adults than just their parents. Again, it was experience that affected judgement. The mothers who expressed this view had in common the experience of seeing their children enjoy the company of other adults. They included white indigenous mothers whose relatives and friends were an important part of the child's social life and mothers from a range of countries who lived in an extended family here or saw it as a normal environment for child-rearing, and for living.

> *M*: 'I think it's important that he has more than me to have a relationship with, yes, that's life actually and it's important – I've tried to do that because my flat mate who used to live here sees a lot of him and often takes him out together and she has spent a whole day with him and I've spent a night away from him now, so I've done that. So he is not just totally dependent on me.'
> *I*: 'Anything else that you do?'
> *M*: 'Yes, I do cultivate it, people who take an interest in him you know, if they're quite happy with James, I tend to like that, and to gravitate towards them. Adults who don't I don't.'
> *I*: 'Any difficulties in providing that?'
> *M*: 'No, I think I'm quite lucky really, because when we do go on

holiday to the farm there's children there, there's lots of adults around there with children and generally my flat mate, quite regularly, Julia, and he sees a friend of Ian's who's around quite regularly and I think that's nice, a mixture of men and women and they take him out to play ball with them. I think people in the street, they say hello James, and wave to him and he's very sociable anyway, he sort of goes to people in buses — but he does have deeper relationships with adults than that, which is nice really.'

These views about how under-2s enjoy, need and benefit from being with a group of other children (and adults) are somewhat different from those of health visitors, as we shall see. It is worth pausing here to consider the ideas that seem to lie behind the mothers' statements.

First and foremost: in expressing these points mothers were clearly not constructing justifications for 'dumping' their children. Mothers expressed sorrow and frustration when they felt they had to leave their children for too many hours, or if they thought the day-care placement was poor in quality; but these were separate issues from their observation that group experience was good for the child. This fits in with their perception (discussed in Chapter 2) of their child as an active, and interactive learner, delighted to explore and interact with both the physical and social environment. The role of the parent here is to provide the child with opportunities to take part in social life, while also taking into account the child's need to spend some time with one or both parents. Mothers are proposing here a theory about the nature of childhood and child development; a theory that emphasizes the child as a social being who both enjoys and learns from the company of other people.

HEALTH VISITORS' PERSPECTIVES

The normal family

The normal family conjured up in the speeches of many politicians (of all persuasions) and assumed in many policy documents is a household with a father in full-time work, a mother as full-time housewife, and children. Fathers are breadwinners who may help at home if their working hours permit; mothers are the care-givers of children (and, in some perspectives, of men too), and they also do the housework. As many people have pointed out, this model is a reality for a minority of households. In households with school-age children, two-thirds of married women and one-half of lone mothers go out to work; where there are under-5s, 28% of mothers work (General Household Survey, 1985, 1987). Twenty-one per cent of mothers of under-2s are in paid work (Moss, 1986). In addition, sizeable proportions of children live in one-parent households, 13% at any one time (Brown, 1988), but far more at some point in their childhood. In our pluralist, multi-ethnic society, some children live in other types of households: with grandparents, and other relatives, or in second families after adoption, fostering or parental remarriage. While the 'traditional normal' family may be a model and basis for social policy and for practice in Britain, it is by no means universal, even for young children, and many mothers, as we have seen, strain against the social policies that reflect this model. The model supported by ideology is amazingly powerful and long-lived, given how various households are.

The sample health visitors gave many spontaneous accounts of their views on 'the family'; also in the third interview (Q 17) we asked them directly about their views on models of motherhood and fatherhood. It was clear from consideration of all these pieces of data that most health visitors held the view that the best and most natural arrangement was for the two parents to live together with traditional divisions of labour. The main justification for this was given in terms of psychological theory. Children needed one main attachment figure who was continuously present, and the mother, who bore the child and (it was to be hoped) breast-fed her, was the natural care-giver. A few health visitors thought complete role-reversal (of which many had one or two examples on their caseloads) was acceptable for the child's well-being.

This health visitor speaks for many in emphasizing the dangers of more than one (or two) adult carers.

HV: 'I feel that child needs to identify with one person and probably that best person is the mother because the child . . . what I'm saying, I'm saying that there are exceptions, but let us just generalize. I think separations of any length do put the child's development at risk, longer separations in particular. So in an ideal world I think the mother is the best person, there are some *good* seconds.'
I: 'Do you want to say more about the good seconds?'
HV: 'The good seconds . . . er . . . I think a good second is a good childminder or someone who actually lives in the house; the mother is maintaining a career for instance. I think a reverse role can work very

well in some families or even the extended family – a granny figure . . .
that sort of shared care . . . I think probably the more people involved
in that, that mother-figure, two is OK, three you could be in trouble.'

The second (but minor) justification was in terms of the practical-
ities of caring work and paid work in our society. Men earn more; they
do not get paid time off for caring; they are unused to caring. Some
health visitors, especially some of those working in inner London,
recognized the psychological and financial stresses many mothers live
with and also recognized that, in practice, many mothers do and will
go out to work – but they saw this, essentially, as an undesirable
necessity or least worst option. Few health visitors (five London,
three county) seriously questioned the naturalness or desirability of
the traditional model, and they tended in general to take a questioning
stance towards social policies as they construct and affect women and
to perceive mothers as constrained by these processes.

In general, then, health visitors took a consensus view of motherhood. That is, it was best, given their psychological beliefs, and the
way our society is organized, that mothers should be at home with
their pre-schoolers.

As suggested in Chapter 2, health visitors thought there were many
child-care tasks for mothers to perform. The main emphasis was not
on the physical aspects of child-care but on the moral and psychological aspects. Mothers should provide a day with a regular pattern to
it, should encourage the child to accept routines and certain habits;
provide a loving secure environment and should stimulate the child.
Her other major ongoing task was to prepare the child for the next
stage of life. That included both developmental and social (or societal)
stages; these were likely to be problematic. So she should learn what
problems were attached to developmental stages and take steps to
forestall or mitigate these problems. For instance, 2 year olds are
likely to have temper-tantrums. She should prepare the child for entry
to play groups, nursery school and then for primary school, by
teaching the child the skills that would be needed, such as the names
of colours, how to tie shoe-laces and socializing with peers. Then the
child would be ready to meet the challenges presented by social and
educational environments. Perhaps most important to note in all this,
is that the mother should make these activities the main focus of her
life.

Health visitors' perceptions of their role with mothers

We discussed in Chapter 2 how most of the health visitors assumed that their own perspectives on the care of young children constituted factual knowledge; where mothers' views differed, those views must in the last analysis be wrong. Health visitors also saw themselves as educators, aiming at improving mothers' child-care standards. These two points may go some way to explaining the most distressing finding in our present study: that many health visitors thought poor characteristics for the work of mothering were common among mothers as a group. We note this point because it was so striking and because it seems important to consider the views of health visitors about those to whom they offer help, advice and information. There is evidence from other studies that other groups of workers, such as social workers and teachers, sometimes denigrate those whom they serve (some judges are rather judgemental too!) (Popay *et al.*, 1986; Prout, 1986).

This health visitor is representative of many. She starts by referring to material problems, but quickly moves on to poor personal orientation towards child-care.

I: 'Thinking about it from a parent's point of view, what do you think are the main problems parents face in bringing up their children healthily? I'm thinking about under-2s.'
HV: 'Under 2?'
I: 'Yes.'
HV: 'I think housing problems. I haven't seen too much of un-employment, the few that I've got that are unemployed are unemploy-able anyway, I think the parents wanting to spend a lot of money on say videos and a lot of money on cigarettes, so that they are unable to spend money on food and the small things that they could – say – in looking after their children. It doesn't cost anything to put the baby in the pram and go for a walk on a nice day such as this, but some of the parents that I visit wouldn't do it, they would sit there in front of the television on an afternoon like this, smoking one cigarette after another.'
I: 'And do you see it as your job to try to help with the problems they have?'
HV: 'Oh yes. I don't think I've said all the problems they face.'
I: 'Well do you want to say some more?'
HV: 'I said housing, spending money appropriately is a bit of a problem, the £100 Christmas present.'
I: 'Are there other problems that they face in bringing up their children?'

HV: 'Yes the fact that they don't particularly want them as children. Well they like children but they don't like the fact that the children are there all the time and they don't have a break from them. A lot of mothers in fact find that almost impossible to cope with and that's why they shut them upstairs or they kick them outside and they are playing out on the road. I think it's the fact that the children are there all the time, although they are not against their children as such. I think they find it a lot to cope with alone and there's no break from it and that is very stressful for some parents, although other parents like having their children around them all the time and they are good mums. I think, yes, I think that's about it.'

I: Of these problems that you give, do you see it as your job to help with them, and which aspects/problems can you help with and which can't you help with and why?'

HV: 'I think one can only go along and make suggestions as to what they should do with the children, like suggesting they go out for a walk on a nice afternoon. If I'm there and they are all in front of the television and smoking and the mother is complaining about how unruly the children are always crying I say, "Well it's a nice day why don't you go out for a walk this afternoon." Whether they will or not is . . . often they say they will but I'm not sure whether they will actually get up and go out. I suppose they just get caught in a rut and it's – they just can't be bothered to do anything. I can make suggestions, I can make suggestions about how they occupy the children, but that in itself means their time and their getting involved with the children and that is not what they want.'

A few of the health visitors (five county, three London) stood out from the rest in that they were *not* judgemental. That is they offered very few comments that blamed mothers. Their line was that individual mothers might have virtues and vices as the rest of us do, but these were not the concern of the health visitor; they did not describe mothers as a group many of whom are likely to have poor characteristics. But most health visitors did seem to think in these terms. Common characteristics ascribed to mothers were: they were over-anxious, did not care, lacked confidence, were easily led, were poorly motivated, were immature, lacked forethought and forward planning abilities and were too closely involved with the child to see objectively. Such words and phrases crop up distressingly often in health visitors' accounts of their work. While some health visitors offered both non-judgemental and blaming comments fairly evenly, there was unfortunately a large group who spoke almost exclusively about mothers in the derogatory ways listed above. They were half of the London health visitors and a third of the county health visitors.

Few health visitors offered praise of mothers. Those who did, referred to them as coping well, doing their best for their children, putting them first.

Health visitors set their comments in an explanatory framework. Almost all thought that poor characteristics and behaviour resulted from 'the cycle of deprivation'. The idea that people pass on from one generation to another orientations to life in general and to child-rearing in particular, is attractive and convincing, superficially. The concept of this remorseless cycle was given prominence in the early 1970s by Keith Joseph who specifically argued for the education of 'parents' to break this cycle. A whole series of studies was commissioned to study the topic; an excellent summary of the evidence is given by Rutter and Madge (1976). Whilst we cannot go into the subject in detail, we recommend that health workers think critically about the concept. Essentially Rutter and Madge argue that people's behaviours are structured and influenced by many factors: such as past experience, material and socioeconomic factors, personality, genetic and biological factors; and though research suggests some intergenerational continuities, it also shows that many people do not reproduce patterns of behaviour and life-styles. We would add that behaviour judged as poor by some onlookers, can instead be interpreted as adaptive behaviour. Thus mothers who smoke are trying to make motherhood bearable and to rally their forces to do a good job of mothering (Graham, 1987). Here is one health visitor, representative of many, talking about the cycle of deprivation and her role in trying to break it:

I: 'What do you think brings about good health?'
HV: 'What brings about good health? Well, I think . . . obviously, the right food, and nourishment. Physical things. And sleep as well, I think that's quite important. Not that every child needs a lot of sleep, but that . . . sleep and routine. So I think that children do need discipline, I think that's all part of good health . . . so that therefore you know . . . a routine. That's for physical health. And of course included in that would be an immunization programme, very much a part of good health, I feel that. Emotionally, I feel . . . emotional health is all a part of good health: a stable relationship with the child, whether that be one parent or two parents, but a stable relationship with really consistent handling, I think – with a lot of love but with discipline, routine, discipline as well. And then the intellectual aspect: that the child needs, again, stimulating; because all these things are interacted. And, you know, part of loving a child is playing with him or her and stimulating . . . and you know since I've been in

(this area) . . . I just feel that there are so many children in insecure families, where the parents are damaged themselves, and you can see the cycle being repeated and . . . I feel somehow as health visitors we've got to try to break that cycle. My own feeling is that we maybe ought to sort of . . . try a different method; I mean, people are very keen about . . . a different approach to our work in many ways . . .'

I: 'Do you want to say more about that?'

HV: 'Well, before . . . Management, a change came about. We did discuss it, the Bristol Project; things like monitoring for cot death, and that sort of thing; and the health visitors here were quite keen to try the Bristol Method. And in a way I feel we need . . . it would be good to try a very set programme, so that the parents know that we're going on to another step, and I feel maybe this approach is worth trying . . . I do feel it's a very, very needy area, with a lot of . . . alcohol and drug abuse, and a lot of young parents who've not been . . . nurtured themselves. Obviously I get a case . . . a lot of work comes in to me, so I probably get a very jaundiced picture . . . but I just feel that there are so many people like that in (this area) . . . and that we're . . . all the resources are just propping it up, and we're not actually, we're not you know actually breaking and stopping that sort of cycle, you know. And that the children of today we don't want to be the deprived parents of tomorrow.'

The health visitors perceived themselves as helping mothers acquire better orientations towards caring for their children. An important part of this was getting mothers to adjust to full-time motherhood – difficult for some mothers, but to be promoted except where mothers were really miserable and giving really bad care. Mothers had to learn to subdue their own needs and identity (and their past) and put their children's needs first. An example of this view was given earlier (Chapter 2, p. 29) where the health visitor assumed that mothers in a group with their children should not talk to each other but only with the children. The idea that mothers might need or like to talk to adults (even given the difficulties of holding a conversation with children present) was unacceptable to her.

A second strand in the health visitor's role was in 'supporting' the mother. This meant giving recognition to the mother that life with children, and especially in poor housing, in the city, in poverty, was difficult, but getting the mother to give good care nevertheless. In addition, some health visitors said they spent a lot of time trying to help with housing, benefits and so on, but since there was little they could guarantee here, the main effort was directed towards helping the mother give good child-care within her current circumstances.

Alternative care: minders, nurseries, informal groups

It will be clear from the foregoing that most health visitors did not see care at minders and nurseries as good for the young child, except as second-best if the mother was desperate to go out to work. In general, the child should be with its mother continuously. That relationship was the only one, essentially, that mattered. The child, at least up to age 2, and for many health visitors up to age 3, was not a social being who played with and formed relationships with other children and adults. Up to age 2 the child engaged in parallel play only.

On the other hand, groups where mothers *had* to stay, that is mother and toddler groups, were a good thing, praised by almost every health visitor. Basically this was because the ideology behind them fitted with that endorsed by most health visitors: that children were not 'ready' to leave their mothers till age 3. Furthermore, for many health visitors (as for the Pre-School Playgroups Association (PPA), the umbrella organization) mother and toddler groups, and later on play-groups, were there to teach mothers how to be good mothers – to interact with their children.

In practice mothers in our sample did not like mother and toddler groups. As we said, mothers needed substantial amounts of time, and reliable time away from their children, to work or to get on with other activities. Some mothers found the unfriendliness of other mothers chilling, as the quotation on pp. 42–43 shows.

This mother's view that she wanted proper day-care was echoed by many and the unfriendliness of the English was also a common theme. An indigenous white mother in a professional job also found oppressive the attempt to incorporate her into a consensus world of women.

I: 'And what about at the doctor's and the clinic? Do you find those easy, friendly places to go to?'
M: 'Sometimes I do and sometimes I don't. I find – I think I'm a bit antisocial actually, I think I'm a bit – like when I had her in the hospital, the delivery room and everything, the birth, was really good, I was really pleased with it, but I'm very bad at this kind of club philosophy – do you know what I mean? Am I making sense here?'
I: 'Yes.'
M: 'I get tremendously sort of cross when people try and involve me in these, in this great club sort of spirit, we're all mothers together or whatever, and that's something that's quite strong in hospitals, you know nurses, they're always very matey and it really quite depressed me afterwards, you know I had a terrible sort of time and I just couldn't

get out of the hospital quick enough and I couldn't feed properly and everything and the dreadful midwives were giving me all this jolly hockey sticks.'

I: 'Were you in long?'

M: 'Six days I was in for, partly because the feeding wasn't going very well and these midwives kept saying, "You know this is just not working out properly". Finally this Australian paediatrician came in and sort of said, "I don't know what all this fuss is about, she can go home". And the nurses still didn't want me to go home, but I just said "Oh I'm going up."

M: 'Was this the X hospital?'

I: 'No, it was Y. And in the same way sometimes the clinic gets me like that, you know they have all these sort of toddlers' groups in there and the 2 o'clock club which is, I don't know, you'll laugh probably because of my situation here, but there's something middle class, white middle class about it. I mean I know I slot very nicely into that situation, but at this stage in time I find it very difficult – it's partly sort of – and that's what I find difficult about the nursery as well, because the teachers and mothers are like that, and I almost feel quite isolated because I'm not particularly into this wholemeal passion and this great breastfeeding thing. I mean I use a dummy and things like that, so that all this sort of thing, I bottle fed and I used a dummy and I used to go into the toddler club down there and feel really quite intimidated by these women . . . I got a letter saying, "If you're a new mum, and you fancy coming along, we're at so and so", but I didn't find it very friendly and I didn't really like it. And I think if you are isolated I'm not sure that it would really – I mean you need a really sort of warm and I don't find them very warm places, I don't find the 2 o'clock club a warm one.'

Some health visitors also recognized the cliquiness and exclusive behaviour of 'in' mothers. But many interpreted mothers' reluctance to go to these groups in terms of individual pathology – they were poorly motivated, did not put the children's needs first, and lacked confidence. For instance:

I: 'Do you think they need help on . . . you suggested things like mixing, going to mothers and toddlers' groups . . .'

HV: 'I think they often do, because it's quite . . . a difficult thing to actually push your way into a group. I mean, I think that's difficult for a lot of people. And so they often I think do need help, to be introduced into a group, they certainly need factual information, but quite often . . . especially with single mums, young, quite shy . . . that they need to be actually introduced to the group leader and you know . . . I think that's important.'

I: 'And do some parents have difficulties giving . . . their children good social contacts, and why?'

HV: 'Yeah. I suppose it's convincing the . . . parent . . . of the importance of it, really. Sometimes distance – quite a long way to a group, and it might be a young mother, you know, who might not be motivated to walk that far . . . Or they just, even if you introduce them into a group, they will just find it difficult to mix . . . the parent might find it very difficult to mix, and not really . . . persevere, you know; I think a lot of people find that quite difficult.'

CLINICAL MEDICAL OFFICERS' PERSPECTIVES

The clinical medical officers offered a mainly technical and responsive (rather than interventionist) service, from their seat in the clinic (*see* Chapter 2). They dealt with people who 'presented' themselves to them. And they almost all consciously distanced themselves from the social and economic circumstances of these 'presenters'.

Some of the 11 doctors accepted uncritically the model of motherhood endorsed in social policies. Mothers' full-time presence was critical for the child's emotional development, certainly for under-3s. Fathers were barely mentioned at all. Essentially these doctors were accepting what they saw in front of them as unproblematic: the people they saw were mothers with children; it was obvious that mothers should be with children. The doctors who challenged this model were, strikingly, those whose experience of other societies provided them with models of the extended family.

Similarly, some of the doctors accepted the common assumption that group care for under-3s was essentially preventive. It gave mothers a break so they would function better as mothers, and compensated children from homes where mothers could not manage mothering. However, others, and again some of the strongest speakers were those with other models to draw on, saw advantages for children in group experience: groups were educative; children learned language, and social skills. These doctors' views were more in accordance with those of most mothers.

Tentatively, we may suggest that the link between some doctors and most mothers here is their common perception of the child as an individual person, with a capacity for social and educational experiences, independent of his or her relationship with the mother. This contrasts with the overwhelming impression given by health visitors, that the small child is an inseparable part of a mother–child dyad and all its important experiences take place in that context. A possible explanation for the doctors' perspective is that the focus of their work, like that of mothers, is directly on the child; whereas the health visitor works with the mother for the child.

FATHERS AND HEALTH WORKERS

Finally, we turn to fathers. As noted above the doctors barely mentioned them. They occupy a minor place as the objects, or subjects of health visitors' attention. This is a topic worth looking at because it raises some interesting issues.

First, preventive child health services are structured very much on the assumption that a 'parent' can come to the clinic or be seen at home during standard working hours (9ish–5ish) and some services are offered between a still shorter range of hours, say 2–4 p.m. on some days. Historically and to a large extent now they are services designed for full-time *mothers*. So health service staff are not readily available to be seen by parents who do paid work – some mothers and most fathers. In practice then, health visitors and doctors do not meet men much.

In another sense, too, the service is not oriented towards fathers. They are perceived as less important care-givers than mothers – a viewpoint which squares with fathers' own views and that of social policies – so they are perceived as less appropriate objects of advice and health education. Thus there is little contact between health visitors and fathers, a point supported by the fact that of our 12 fathers, five did not know the health visitor well enough to say whether she was good or not. In the county area, the health visitors, in their account of their work, almost never mentioned fathers: men there are not 'naturally' visible: they work long hours away from home, many commuting long distances. However, some London health visitors did talk about fathers; they were seeing more now, they said, because of high unemployment and because some fathers were taking more interest in child-care and so came to clinic or sat in on home visits. A few (4) thought it was important for health visitors to see fathers, in order to understand both adults' perspectives and to be better equipped to give appropriate health education.

> *HV*: 'You'd get a much more balanced view of the family obviously. Each person has their own insight into that child and into the needs of their family. I mean if you only have one side of it it could be quite out of

balance and also if you are hoping to influence ways of behaviour in a family, you're doing a more effective job if you are speaking to both sides of the same family.'

Some London health visitors (11 of 28) saw fathers as a problem: they rejected the health visitor (by leaving the room or ostentatiously reading the paper!), were critical or rejecting of what she said, or were seen as potentially or actually violent.

Another difficulty health visitors (and interviewers) may face is the relationship of men they meet in households to the mother or child. How do you establish (if you feel you should) what this biological or emotional relationship is, and how do you approach to question whether fathers or boyfriends or house husbands should be interested in child-care? Some health visitors also felt uneasy about asking about father's employment status.

(The health visitor is decribing a home visit: Q 3.)

HV: 'I arrived at the door. As I was going in there were two young men. I thought one was perhaps the father, but I wasn't sure because I haven't met him before. I knew the mother very well, no problem getting in, she quite likes me to go and I walked in and the 2 year old met me, and that was fine. I realized that the two young chaps – one was the mother's brother and one was the husband and the husband didn't take any part in the – '

I: 'Although he was present?'

HV: 'He wasn't, he actually left the room. The previous time I was around he was in the kitchen next door, and this time I thought he might actually come in because the mother's brother was in the room but he actually stayed out, so I am a bit worried about that, he's not taking much – he probably does take an interest in the children, but he probably feels that it is a woman's world or something with me going around and he didn't take any part at all, but on questioning the mother he seems to be helping a bit with the children, but it was a bit difficult because he was next door. We were discussing mainly the problem about the 2 year old with the baby. The baby was fine she was feeding alright and settling down alright, the 2 year old had been playing up a bit mainly towards the parents, and her potty training also re-gressed . . .'

(Health visitor goes on to describe baby-care advice she gave. Then the interviewer introduces a prompt.)

I: 'And did you feel happy about the child-care in the house?'

HV: 'Yes, apart from the fact that the father wasn't taking any obvious part – but that is very difficult really to just go visiting.'

I: 'Have you ever raised that?'

HV: 'No, because he was employed before and he has been there the last two times I have been that he has been next door in the kitchen so I wasn't able to bring it up. I was going to in fact today if he hadn't arrived back, but he did, so it was no good.'

I: 'You think he is unemployed?'

HV: 'Yes, definitely unemployed now, that is quite a recent thing, yes. In fact the previous time I had asked if he was helping, but I hadn't realized he was next door in the kitchen and she said yes and pulled a face. What was really happening, I will ask about that next time.'

I: 'Do you feel that if there are two parents in a household that you should be talking to both?'

HV: 'Yes, I try to.'

I: 'So what will you do do you think?'

HV: 'Yes, I will go again in a couple of weeks or so and try to ask about the husband helping again. Hopefully she might come to the clinic and I am sure he won't come and that might be a good chance to speak to her on her own and say "How are things really now he is un-employed?" Because it is a very recent thing.'

Clearly men present a problem to a domiciliary service staffed mainly by women. Some health visitors talked about the difficulties posed by incidents when a man answered the door. Some authorities advise staff not to interview on their own.

DISCUSSION

Working with mothers

In this and the previous chapters we have set out some of the most dramatic contrasts our study provides: between the perspectives of mothers on the one hand and of health visitors on the other, regarding parenthood and early childhood and child-care. It is, as we suggested, not surprising that these two groups should differ. They have different knowledge-bases, different experiences and different sorts of child-care work.

It's worth noting that the experience of bringing up their own children was not a factor that affected health visitors' views on how mothers should spend their time – or on any other topic. It seems that when in role as a health visitor, they were more affected by dominant ideologies in health visiting, than by experiential knowledge as mothers.

The differences in perspectives between mothers and health

visitors may be interesting in themselves. They also perhaps serve as clues why health workers find that mothers do not always accept their suggestions with enthusiasm. When one of us described the data at a meeting recently, a clinical psychologist said our description made him suddenly realize why a mother looked so dubious when he urged the value of working towards long-term goals in child-management; she was concerned with short-term goals as well, such as the child's happiness now!

If mothers' perspectives differ from those of health visitors, then this suggests certain implications for health visitors' work. Important in this work, they said, was education and support. In the next chapter we discuss goals and methods of health education in some detail; here it is worth suggesting that among many other considerations, the health educator may need to take into account the importance of each side being clear about the other's basic goals and values. Otherwise the educator may fail to change the views and behaviour of the educatee. If health visitors aim to support mothers in the work of mothering, it would again seem important that each side understands the values that lead to certain behaviours being classified as 'support'. For instance, the health worker whose goal is 24-hour care by the mother, will seek to help her give that, while for a mother whose goal as a mother is, in part, resourcing the household, will welcome support that consists of enabling her to go out to work.

The work of the health visitor, as presently defined, is therefore difficult and delicate. While doctors, in our limited experience, restrict their work largely to responding to mothers' expressed needs and concerns about the child and child management, but avoid involvement in social and economic issues, the health visitor both adopts a more interventionist style of work and is more exposed to mothers' social and economic problems, because she works in the community. As some health visitors suggested, her work may be most useful to mothers if she starts by trying to understand what mothers' values and problems are and attempts to work *with* mothers to enable them to achieve their goals. However, that is not easy work in a society where mothers perceive so many barriers set against them to prevent them leading a good life with their children.

Fathers

As we said, fathers are seen little by health visitors and hardly at all by doctors. Health service staff may well find it difficult to think about them as possible service-users. However, there are some points worth debating here.

The first point is that since health visitors see themselves (and are seen by the Health Visitors' Association) as family visitors, it can be argued that their services should be directed at male as well as at female parents. If 'families' have fathers as well as mothers, then even if the father's role is more minor than the mother's, fathers may be seen as needing help to be good fathers. As one health visitor said (in connection with suspected child abuse):

> *HV*: 'I suppose that's the biggest problem in an area like this, where there are so many parents like that, is that you can't stretch the . . . budget will only go so far and you can't always give the help you feel that some of them need. I really do feel quite burdened about the young parents who are . . . so damaged themselves. I mean, quite often the young dads . . . you know, they . . . just need mothering themselves. And that's the other thing: that I feel . . . our services are very geared to the mother and *child*, and not to the father necessarily. And my own feelings are that we should try to . . . include fathers in our network much more.'

To go on from that point, some would argue that to offer the best advice, tailored to the characteristics and needs of the individual family the advisor needs to understand family dynamics. The mother's story is surely not enough to go on. Yet while many health visitors thought it would be 'nice', or 'useful' to see fathers, only four London and no county health visitors thought it was important or necessary.

This point becomes acutely relevant when workers become concerned about the physical and/or psychological well-being of the child. It seems problematic for workers in suspected or actual child abuse cases to work only with and through women. Some health visitors gave us examples of attempts made by health visitors and social workers to get mothers to change fathers' behaviour and attitudes. Yet another load for women to bear! (c.f. Brook and Davis, 1985).

It should be noted that changing marital and parental norms means that there is a small but important number of men who rear their children alone. They may be at sea in the world of child-rearing, lack the support of social networks, and find it difficult to use existing services – run by women for women. Yet probably they would welcome services appropriate to their needs.

Finally on the role of the services with fathers, it may be considered desirable that services play their part (however small) in helping to promote equal opportunities for men in the important (and reward-ing) work of child-rearing. Those who plan and provide services may wish to consider how they could be made more accessible to men. More flexible opening hours at clinics would be a start. Group work that focuses on men as fathers may also be relevant.

DISCUSSION TOPICS

1 How should health workers work, given differences they may perceive between their own and parents' perspectives on parent-hood and childhood?
2 What should and can health services staff do to make services accessible to men?

FURTHER READING

Boulton, Mary G. (1983). *On Being A Mother*. London: Tavistock Public-ations. This gives a clear account of a researcher's findings on how women experience motherhood both on a day-to-day basis and in more general terms.
Cohen, B. (1988). *Caring for Children*. Report for the European Commission's Childcare Network. A report on pre-school services in the UK, carried out as part of an EEC study of member states' policies and practices.
David, Miriam (1985). Motherhood and social policy – a matter of education? *Critical Social Policy*; **12**: 28–43. This article gives a wide-ranging account of social policies which aim to confirm women in caring roles, and as better mothers.
Rutter, M. and Madge, N. (1976). *Cycles of Deprivation*. London: Heinemann. A comprehensive analysis and discussion of evidence and issues.

CHAPTER 4
CHILD SURVEILLANCE AND HEALTH EDUCATION

The welfare of children is of interest to many people – parents, health workers, teachers and social workers. In this chapter we explore the role of health visitors in overseeing the health and welfare of these future citizens. We shall consider the health visitors' perception of their role in policing, monitoring and educating parents as care-takers of children. We shall pay particular attention to the supervision and health education of mothers since health visitors identified these as important aspects of their work.

Issues raised in this chapter include:

- in a society which both believes in the freedom of the individual, and wants to ensure that children are given a certain level of care, what type and level of surveillance of parental child-care standards are acceptable?
- what models of health education should health workers use?
- can health visitors reconcile the two roles of surveillance and health education?

We shall consider the perspectives of mothers and of health visitors on intervention and health education, but before doing so, we look at the work situation of health visitors and more importantly at the constraints which they, and many other health workers, experience in delivering services. We start by considering briefly the historical baggage of health visiting, and go on to note how their work is defined for them by others as well as by working conditions. These can impose limitations on the achievements of health visitors.

CONTEXT OF HEALTH VISITING

Historical inheritance of health visiting

The history of health visiting is closely linked to the gradual development of state intervention in matters of health (Dingwall, 1982; Robinson, 1982). In the field of preventive health two new occupations emerged: the public sphere of environmental health became the concern of a mainly male work-force – public health or environmental health officers. In that field environmental and social factors are identified as the cause of ill health and preventive measures are reinforced through legislation.

In personal preventive health, women were identified as carers of men and children (David, 1985). Women workers were employed to oversee and modify the behaviour of other women as mothers and wives. This area of preventive health work rests on the premise that individual behaviour can importantly affect health status and that people should take more responsibility for their health than they are thought to do. Workers here attempt to 'educate' and change the behaviour of people. Health visiting is still predominantly a female occupation and mothers remain the target group for health education (Chapter 3). Whilst in the field of public health there are legal sanctions, in preventive health care there is no back-up in law. Workers such as health visitors have to *negotiate* access to people. They operate between the public sphere – state interest in the health of its future generations – and the private sphere of home and motherhood (Stacey and Davies, 1983).

In the early days health visitors – usually from the middle classes – were employed to teach mothers – usually from the working classes – the 'rules' of hygiene and nutrition. Teaching and changing the behaviour of mothers remains a major role of health visitors. More recently, however, health education has been extended to encompass emotional and social aspects as well as physical aspects of health and these 'health topics' often involve moralistic values (*see* Chapters 2 and 3). With the recent increase in public and official recognition of child abuse, health visitors have also become increasingly concerned with inspecting households to detect and prevent ill treatment of children.

The work of health visitors with young children therefore stems from the view that the health of the future citizens of this country is not a purely private affair but is also a public issue. To oversee the well-being of these children, health visitors need to intervene in the private world of child-rearing. By intervention we mean any unsolicited action taken by health visitors to concern themselves with the way parents bring up their children. The home visit is a good example of intervention since in some cases workers call unannounced and feel it is legitimate to visit households with young children to maintain surveillance and educate parents. An opposite to that would be a service which only responds to calls for help from parents.

Social construction of the role of health visitors

For people like health visitors, especially for those who are employees, their work and the form it takes is to a large extent defined by others. Historical traditions, official social policies, dominant beliefs and ideologies about health, demands of employing authorities and managers, those of educational establishments, all help to influence and determine the tasks deemed to be appropriate for the individual worker. The 'autonomy' of the field-worker to organize her work is highly constrained by expectations of her. The various bodies which influence the role of the worker may not even be in agreement. In the case of health visitors, educational institutions and managers of employing authorities may impose conflicting interpretations of the role of the field-worker (McClymont, 1980). So the social and historical construction of their work may to a large extent shape workers' views of their work.

Working conditions of health visitors

As with all employees, the work of the health visitor is either hindered or facilitated by their working conditions which depend on their employing authorities, for example, staffing levels, office accommodation, clerical back-up and support.

Almost all the health visitors we interviewed expressed some dissatisfaction with their working conditions (Table 4.1). Only four London and one county health visitor had no complaints at all. The level of dissatisfaction among health visitors ranged from those who were unhappy with most aspects of their working conditions to some who expressed minor discontent.

There were, as we expected, differences between the County and

Table 4.1 Health visitors' views on their working conditions

Main problems described	London n = 28	County n = 20
Unable to do enough home visits	10	1
Impossible to carry out health authority guidelines	7	0
Insufficient or no clerical support	14	7
Insufficient staffing level	10	9
Inadequate office accommodation	5	10

Note: Some health visitors described more than one problem.

the London health visitors in the social context in which they operated. Whilst the County health visitors worked in areas with few 'social problems', most of the London health visitors were confronted daily with serious social problems: inadequate housing, unemployment and poverty. Their patches included areas of wealth, but the general picture they saw was one of urban decay, deprivation and disadvantage. In the county area, there were small pockets of disadvantage in the midst of fairly affluent to very affluent households. So, the London health visitors saw themselves as working with a stressed and needy population, whereas the County health visitors did not. Their pattern of work was thus affected. In describing their work during the previous week only one-quarter (5) of the County health visitors talked of dealing with households experiencing major problems, whilst over half (18) of the London health visitors reported doing so. The nature of the 'problems' also differed, with county health visitors reporting mainly problems in personal relationships, while London health visitors were dealing with situations such as drug addiction, prison sentence, violence, alcoholism, homelessness and extreme poverty. Many felt submerged by crisis work and were unable to follow the guidelines issued by the health authority.

(London health visitor talking about her caseload:)
'. . . but (children) over a year unless they have got severe problems I don't see them because I really don't have the time, I have got 18 on health recall (households considered to be "at risk") at the moment and we are supposed to see them monthly or at least have contact with them monthly but a social worker has a caseload of 25 so I think it is very difficult to give what you feel is adequate care for the families that you are supposed to be visiting. When I first started I felt very, very pressurized and I didn't think I was going to be able to cope then I realized that I can only do as much as I am capable of doing and I am not satisfied with what I am doing. . . .'

She went on to say that 'management didn't have any conception of what the work was like'. Many London health visitors spoke in these terms, and a few county health visitors also felt highly pressurized, especially in one particular area where there was a shortage of staff, because (we were told) the price of housing was too high for health service staff.

Many health visitors complained of inadequate office space, as do those in other studies (e.g. Draper *et al.*, 1983). This was mainly a problem of the county area, especially for health visitors cramped into inadequate general practice accommodation. Two London health visitors who were attached to general practitioners complained of the time spent travelling. In the county area, only four health visitors complained of too much travelling, although many more gave accounts of spending much time travelling; they appeared to accept this as a normal part of the job.

Health visitors identified two major hindrances to good work: shortage of staff, which led to very large caseloads, and too much administrative work. These reduced the amount of time they spent doing 'real' health visiting: that is, home visits. Guidelines issued by managers also imposed constraints. For example county health visitors said they were told that under-5s constituted a priority and this reduced the time they could spend with other age groups.

It is crucial when considering the perspectives of workers to keep in mind the context in which they operate. Here we have argued that the constraints within which health visitors deliver a service affects both the practice of their work and their perspectives. We now consider two major aspects of their role and raise some issues concerning these: child surveillance and health education.

CHILD SURVEILLANCE AND HEALTH EDUCATION

Child surveillance might cover a continuum from the compulsory supervision of households to ensure that children are not being ill treated, through monitoring their health, to promoting the development of the child's full potential. It is instructive to consider other countries, for example France, where the state obliges parents as guardians of future citizens to subject their children to certain health measures. In the UK no such compulsion exists. Nevertheless, workers are given the task to oversee the well-being of children. Employees such as health visitors and social workers provide their services in a situation, where society expects them to ensure the well-being of children but which also emphasizes the personal freedom of parents. There is a tension here which social workers, health visitors and the police have to face and work with. This tension may be unavoidable and may even be desirable. The conflict which results can be seen as a positive feature of a democratic society. In the field of child surveillance factors considered to be desirable are constantly negotiated between interested parties. The recent Cleveland case provides an example (Campbell, 1988).

Mothers may not share the outlook of health and social workers. In a society divided by class, culture and ethnicity, there are many models of good health care. Mothers' ideas may vary and may also differ from those of paid workers. As we suggested in Chapter 2 mothers and paid workers bring different sets of experiences and interests to child-care. Another difference is that while mothers have the interest of a particular child at heart, the aim of paid workers is to cover a whole child population. This plurality and difference in perspectives could be a source of conflict between paid and unpaid workers.

The service of health visitors in the UK is interventionist and is offered (at least in theory) on universalist principles. Mothers welcome some aspects of the services, but may also object to what they see as an infringement of their freedom to rear children as they wish.

MOTHERS' PERSPECTIVES

We now look at the comments from mothers in our sample about intervention and health education. When considering the child preventive services we need to remember that services include elements both of benevolence and of control. Health visitors made it clear that in both health education and surveillance work those were two motive elements. It was obvious to us that they wanted to help mothers do a good job because they were genuinely concerned with the long-term well-being of children. Running in tandem with this was an element of control. Health visitors may not recognize this but we think it is an important motive. They attempted to control the mothers' actions and watched the outcome of mothers' child-care practices. Mothers, even if at times feeling the sharp edge of the control element, recognized benevolence. They appreciated the existence of a health visiting service and many were grateful for the help they had received.

All the parents in our study, except two fathers who were dubious, accepted the element of control. They did not necessarily like to be inspected but they accepted this. They perceived the major role of health visitors to be that of inspecting households to detect child abuse, a view probably encouraged by the media. An exception to this were those mothers who had been in this country for less than 6 years. They viewed the service of health visitors as help offered to parents to bring up their children well, but other parents saw the health visitor's role as essentially ensuring that children are not abused.

> *I*: 'Can I ask you why you think health visitors come round?'
> *M*: 'Why they come round? Well, you hear so many bad things about what people do. I think why they come to your house is to check up, to make sure your baby's healthy . . . and that you're treating it right, which is a good thing. And sometimes you think, "Oh no", if you want to go out and they're sort of coming, but then I think how some children are treated, I think it's a good idea.'

> (Mother commenting on the fact that she had not seen her health visitor for a very long time:)
> 'I suppose she's obviously been to me and she's seen that really I'm quite a good parent and everything. Andrew is always nice looking and the place is usually pretty tidy, I mean it's not spotless (laughing), but there's no dirt or anything. It's usually his toys everywhere . . . maybe she should come more often you know, because maybe I could be one of these mothers. Although I keep the place, I mean I could be beating the hell out of the baby. But then I suppose . . . it's better for her to go to somebody who does need her than rather come to me because I don't really need a health visitor.'

We turn now to mothers' views of health education by health visitors and here it is important to remember two points about mothers' knowledge (*see* Chapter 2). First, they had access to information from a range of sources: family, friends, the media and health workers including health visitors.

> *I*: 'Is the health visitor useful to you now?'
> *M*: '. . . if anything is wrong with Jane, I'd ring my family more than I'd ring the health visitor, because they know her better than she does. I suppose she's (the health visitor) not really much good to me in that way, but I suppose if there is anything to do with the clinic or anything like that, I would get in touch with her.'

Secondly, they were now confident about their own knowledge gained mainly by getting to know the child.

> *I*: 'Is the health visitor useful to you now?'
> *M*: 'Well, not a lot because he is grown up now . . . when the baby is small then you need the help. But when they grow up, then you get used to it — and you know what to do.'

This knowledge and confidence form the basis for mothers' belief that they should initiate discussion about health and child-care topics. They appreciated access to health workers, but felt that it was for them to judge when to seek advice. They did not accept that health visitors had a right to give unsolicited advice. We think this is a most striking and important finding which has implications for health workers. It is supported by other studies (Mayall, 1986; McIntosh, 1987).

> *I*: 'Health visitors come to families with a baby or a small child and ask to come in and talk with you. Do you think that's all right?'
> *M*: 'Yes, I don't mind as long as they don't start telling you what you should be doing, especially if they have not got any children of their own, which I know she has not, sometimes they start saying, "you should be doing this."'

The methods and styles of health education adopted by health workers were critical in determining the willingness of mothers to take note of their messages. Mothers appreciated health visitors who gave them time, listened to them and discussed topics raised by them.

> *I*: 'What do you see as being her (health visitor's) job?'
> *M*: 'Well I don't know exactly but I know whenever I have some problem, anything, and she really discusses and gives me a lot of time and gives me advice. It's good. I like it because with the doctors it's very difficult to discuss problems, they don't have so much time.'

The manner and the attitude of the health visitor as adviser were also important. As the following comments suggest mothers liked a non-directive non-didactic approach and a discussion between equals.

> (Mother comparing two health visitors, the present one whom this mother liked and a previous one whom she did not like.)
> '. . . we sort of hit if off. I think because she was very . . . she did not force anything down me. She did not come out with advice which the other health visitor had done and had kind of made little comments

which made me feel I was not doing the right thing or how stupid I was to have thought so and so. She did not come out with anything moralistic. It was very nice.'

I: 'Health visitors come to families with a young child and ask to come and talk with you. Do you think that's all right?'

M: 'It depends really, some of them have got an appalling attitude, this is from talking to other people and I don't know whether it's just personality or whatever . . . I think it depends on what kind of attitude they have. I mean the mere fact that they've got a right to come in and talk . . . I mean they should really leave it to the individual. But on the other hand, one could argue that not everybody is going to know they need a health visitor . . . I really don't know . . . I think that it's assuming people who need health visitors don't know the difference and implies something about their intelligence.'

To sum up, mothers liked genuine exchange of views based on respect for them as responsible people, and respect for their views and their autonomy. They accepted that health visitors should inspect households to prevent child abuse and saw this as a major function of health visitors.

HEALTH VISITORS' PERSPECTIVES

Generally health visitors did not question the appropriateness of intervention. As one said, 'I don't think about it, I just do it, that's my job – that is to offer the services to any family with under-5s, the handicapped and the elderly.' The health visitor's job is defined for her by the profession and by managers and includes home visiting as a major feature. Most thought an important purpose of the home visit was to educate mothers.

The major reason health visitors gave for intervening in the private sphere of the family was that they were advocates for children, representing the child on behalf of society. As child's advocate the health visitor's work involved not only protecting the child from abuse but also ensuring that the child was given all opportunities to achieve her full potential. It was very clear to them that, at the end of the day, their job was to protect children. They saw this as justifying any amount and type of intervention they thought necessary. However, they construed this work as benevolent rather than controlling work, because it was for the protection of children. The health visitors' argument was: child-rearing is a difficult task; essentially intervention is justified and necessary because parents cannot be trusted to carry out this task. Health visitors, the argument continued, had an essential role in overseeing parental behaviour; they had knowledge, high moral standards, integrity and an accepted supervisory role offered on a universalist basis. Parents, even the best, could not be assumed to have all the knowledge and moral integrity required for the difficult task of child-rearing; they therefore needed constant assessment and reappraisal by health visitors. For some health visitors this stance unfortunately led to derogatory comments on mothers.

Parents were not sufficiently prepared for the experience of having a child:

'I think they need advising about normal children. I think, I mean most of them go into parenthood with less consideration of what it's going to mean than they do into buying a new car, I think they have put less thought sometimes into having a baby . . . I think that particularly first-time parents, they're not very well informed about child-care and about normality and about what to expect and about what to do at certain stages and you know what is normal and what is abnormal.'

In some cases parents were irresponsible. In this next extract the health visitor also shows she has the power to label officially 'on record' the mother as being irresponsible, which she uses to coerce the mother.

(This health visitor is talking about her role in immunization:)
'Promoting as much as possible – always aware of every individual's choice . . . trying to get them to have it at the right times and not to keep putting it off, just for silly little reasons . . . I'll say I don't accept that as an excuse why you did not come. You say it was pouring with rain and that – you know – it's more important health. You have to do that with some families and even taking the tack that you know they're not going to come you say, "don't just say you are going to come to please me. Do you want your child protected or do you want to run the risk of having these diseases?" And being quite forthright. And even to the point of with some families saying, "if you tell me the truth if you are not going to come, I'll write it down there: Mummy's not prepared to come, we won't mention it again." And I think sometimes that spurs them to come. Because they don't actually like you to write down that they've refused something.'

Finally some parents were simply ignorant.

'There are those . . . there are the poor families and the ignorant families where you've got to try and whittle away at the ignorance and give support and advice where you can.'

All health visitors viewed the health education of mothers as a major and intrinsic feature of their work. The strong emphasis they gave to 'educating' mothers was linked to their belief in the power of the individual to achieve good health through 'good behaviour'. Health visitors acknowledged that material factors such as housing and adequate income affected health but emphasized that individuals could and should choose to carry out practices favouring health. We shall explore this topic at greater length in Chapter 7.

It is notable that the majority of health visitors in our study said they carried out what they called 'routine education'. They had a mental list of topics to introduce, often chosen according to the age and the perceived developmental stage of the child. They introduced these topics as a matter of routine. This was a recurrent theme in the accounts they gave us. The general picture of meetings between mothers and health visitors was of health visitors in a dominant role, introducing the topics they chose as important and paying much less attention to *responding* to mothers' requests. This picture is supported by Sefi (1988) in her analysis of conversations between mothers and health visitors.

HV: "Yes I bring up some topics with all families, no matter who they are, because the ones I think know like to hear and the others just listen. You hope it has an effect.'

HEALTH EDUCATION MODELS

Ideas about health education can usefully be seen in the context of the development by WHO, during the 1980s, of the concept of health promotion. As a recent statement puts it:

'Basic resources for health are income, shelter and food. Improvement in health requires a secure foundation in these basics, but also: information and lifeskills; a supportive environment, providing opportunities for making healthy choices among goods, services and facilities; and conditions in the economic, physical, social and cultural environments (the "total" environment) which enhance health' (WHO, 1986).

WHO is promoting programmes world-wide to put the achievement of good health on the agenda of policy-makers and service-providers. People's access to good health is seen to depend on two broad interlinked factors: a healthy environment and the information and skills to choose health-promoting life-styles.

Health educators' approaches to their work depend on their ideas about whose knowledge (that of educator or learner) is relevant to the education process. At a general level, we can identify two main models of education. At one extreme health education is seen as a 'dialogue' of health workers in partnership with people (c.f. Freire, 1972). Here the worker acknowledges the limitations of her own knowledge, and values the knowledge of other people. In this situation the worker may encourage people to think about certain topics but leaves them free to decide a suitable course of action. The educator does not have set and predetermined objectives. The outcome of the encounter is left to the 'learner'. Therefore, here the educator makes no attempt to exert pressure on people to conform to her norms. She respects people's decisions even if these conflict with her personal views. The means used is that of exchanging information and stimulating discussion. Learning, in this model of education, is thought to occur through open, equal-status contributions from both sides and this type of education cannot by definition occur in a covert manner. It requires that both sides actively engage in the educational enterprise. Mothers in our sample generally favoured this model and for health educators, who need the cooperation of people in order to be effective, this model is appropriate and likely to yield good results.

At the other extreme we have 'education from above' or a 'top/down' model. In this case the worker believes that she has the 'right' message and makes strong attempts to change behaviour in line with that message. The worker here acts as an expert and views her knowledge as superior to that of her 'pupils'. The educator has certain predetermined objectives in mind. The aim is to change people to achieve these objectives. At its extreme, this type of 'education' merges into indoctrination; strong pressure is exerted on people to change in certain directions and a high level of control is exerted by the worker. Both an overt and covert manner may be used. A covert 'top/down' approach may try to disguise the fact that this is an authoritarian method of 'education'. This model is less likely to be effective since people's cooperation is needed if their behaviour is to change.

Health education models of health visitors in our study

Very few of the health visitors approximated to a perfect type of one of these two models of education. However, each health visitor could be placed on a continuum between the two extremes. In Table 4.2 we indicate the models of health visitors we interviewed and then give examples of these as illustrations.

Table 4.2 Health education models – health visitors (HVs)

	London HVs (n = 28)	County HVs (n = 20)
Group A	4	2
Group B	13	3
Group C	11	15

Those health visitors (Group A) who believed in true partnership felt strongly that parents had the right to accept or reject their services and that they should respect that right. Health education consisted of exchanging information on an equal footing with mothers.

'When I do a new birth, I always explain to them what the job is, what I have done before and ask them whether they want me to visit them at home or not, give them the choice and I say if they don't want me, they can always ring me up and if they say they do want a visit, I ask them whether they want to come and see me at the clinic. And once you have got all that sorted out you carry on from there.'

Other health visitors (Group B) liked the idea of dialogue and partnership but they also tried to make mothers change in the direction which they identified as correct. The level of intervention and control they exerted depended on how they assessed a given situation. This health visitor belonged to that category:

HV: 'I firmly believe that parents are responsible for the child and I'm there just as help and support and advice, whatever you think – for them to call on, however if they want to use me. Obviously there are certain things that I would think is not healthy for a child. I would explain to the mother why I thought it was not healthy . . . but if she insisted on doing that practice, I'd say, "well after all it's your child", and you know that I don't think that's quite right but I would support her in the right to do what she likes with her child. Within reason, it depends what it is – OK there has to be a point when you have to say, "right this is not healthy practice at all, I cannot allow it to go on. And if you're not going to change that then I'm going to have sort of say to someone that it's a problem". It comes very . . . not very often actually. But sometimes also if they are practising something unhealthy with the child in whatever context, maybe an explanation of why can make them see and they'll say, "I had not thought of it like that". And then go your way. Although I don't like to think of it going my way exactly, but maybe the correct way. But there's very few things that I'm actually adamant on, like you know never prop feeding a child, adding solids to a bottle – I get quite cross about that, but other things they're all . . . it's a matter of opinion, a lot of things anyway.'

But many health visitors fell into the third group (Group C). Their brief was simply to change the behaviour of mothers and to teach them to act in certain ways for the benefit of children. As one health visitor said, 'I feel I have a duty to try and advise mothers for the sake of the child because I feel the child can't sort of speak for itself.'

Some worked covertly and others in an overt manner. Most used a covert style. That is, they worked with a hidden agenda. They told us how in their encounters with mothers they would surreptitiously introduce a topic they believed to be important. These health visitors said that a 'good relationship' with the mother enabled them to introduce unsolicited advice in their intervention.

HV: 'Well the first thing you do is try to build up a relationship, try to get them to trust you, right from the very beginning – although you know I have met the odd ones who say, "yes, yes, yes", and then you've gone back and they've gone back to their same old routine. But then you know, you sort of do one thing at a time; you don't barge in and say . . . take over the whole thing, you just gently do one thing at a time or you wait until the timing is right then you might bring in things like smoking or something like that.'

HV: 'If I see that things are pretty grotty . . . If I think that the mother's got a relationship with me where we can chat about food – I'll say, "what did you have on Sunday, did you have something nice and oh, you had a little party and does the little (child) like this, that or the other". I try to bring it into the conversation, but in a very non-authoritarian way. Really more of a conversation piece. Usually they end up telling *me* things. They tell me what they believe. And you can't always say I think that's not absolutely right, because they'd be offended. But sometimes you can. If you tell them the child is overweight, they won't come to the clinic again! You have to be careful.'

I: 'But do you see it as part of your job to . . .'

HV: 'Yes, I do. I think food's terribly important actually, and diet. It is my job, but do the public see it as my job and if they do see it as my job do they think it's awfully fussy and stupid and I'm old-fashioned and that I won't listen to them. So you have to be with it really and you've got to be clever about it (laughing). I don't think I'd like anyone coming in and tell me what I should be cooking for my children. It's the human angle isn't it, especially when you think you've been doing very well. 'Cos next time I really do want her not to feel I was criticizing her even though she was doing nicely. It's difficult isn't it' (laughing).

These health visitors justified such covert methods for at least two reasons. First, they saw themselves as accountable to society for overseeing the welfare of children and for preventing child abuse; however, they could be denied access to the home if they upset mothers while carrying out their educative role. So they took it gently.

HV: 'I think it's very important how you present yourself, your attitude. You can try and change people without being too . . . I mean if you go in and say, "ooh yes, you mustn't do that" – you just put their back up and they won't listen to you – they won't welcome you.'

Secondly, they were aware that, except in extreme conditions, they were unable to force mothers to behave in a given way. They believed that they might be successful if they went about it in a subtle manner.

HV: 'I think that cow's milk is the big thing at the moment. A lot of mums who perhaps have got a baby off the breast or the bottle tend to offer cow's milk a lot earlier than I would like to see them, so I try to encourage them to leave it as near to the one-year-old mark as possible as an example. Yes, I think it's a bit difficult to lay down the law because I think you have to see what the circumstances are and what is happening and treat it accordingly and not be too inflexible in one's own attitudes even though, you know you'd much rather they did not do a certain thing, 'cos they're all going to go home and do it anyway whatever you've said. But hopefully you'll persuade them that there is a good reason for them doing it differently.'

A few health visitors preferred a direct, overt style of education. Others who generally operated an 'education by stealth' method might use an overt style on some occasions. The examples illustrate also the constant concern of health visitors that they might damage the tenuous relationship between them and mothers.

'I was doing a check at home and bigger brother came and I don't

know they must be boiled sweets wrapped in paper and sister got hold of it. And I said, "Oh", (laughs) I made my remark, I don't know whether I upset her but I did not mean to upset her but I said you know, but in fact we did talk about . . . the girl had eating problems and there you are . . . but you know it's constant – it's constantly they have their ideas, if they haven't, one tries to convey perhaps nice ideas.'
'. . . coming out of the shopping queue and you'll see them with bars of chocolate . . . What do I do? I tell them it's wrong (laughs) . . . They know. As my clinic nurse says you've got the great big hand out over them, now look you know . . . but not, I don't tell them in an aggressive manner . . . There are two ways of saying everything you know. When I say, "Haha, you were at clinic with me last week saying: 'he won't eat,' why are you doing this?" I mean you know this is totally wrong, but you don't, you know there's two ways of saying things.'

However, mothers at times openly challenged the health visitor, as one explained:

'. . . I have talked to some women in the street who broke out the jam doughnuts stuffed the dummy in it, then give it to the baby and they turn to me and say, "you won't like that, will you". So I mean some people know what they are doing is the wrong thing because that's the way they want to do things. Those kinds of mothers there is not much you can do, others might take notice.'

THE PROTECTION OF CHILDREN FROM ABUSE

In recent years there has been increasing public interest in the detection and prevention of child abuse. Violence within households is not a new phenomenon, but increasingly the protection of children is becoming a public issue, where it is seen fit for a growing range of workers to intervene on behalf of children.

Surveillance of children to detect child abuse centres on the rights of the individual child. The protection of children by public employees however, leads to debates about the rights of parents as opposed to those of children. This may result in overt conflict, as in Cleveland.

Health visitors in our sample felt strongly that they had a major role as advocates of children. They represented and defended the rights of children, at times against their parents, on behalf of society. (This role is similar to that of obstetricians as advocates for unborn children.) All health visitors stressed this advocacy role, although some felt uneasy about 'policing' households.

The work experience of the two samples of health visitors differed. All London health visitors had 'cases' of child abuse or households considered to be 'at risk', while many but not all of the county health visitors had come across 'cases' of child abuse. This perhaps explains why county health visitors did not discuss this issue as fully as London health visitors.

Many health visitors believed that in many cases parents who abused their child had themselves been abused as a child (Table 4.3). This theory of a 'cycle of deprivation' was a prevalent explanatory model used by our samples of health visitors to explain other types of parental behaviour, as we discussed in Chapter 3. They also cited both individual failings and environmental factors as causes of child abuse, and several gave both types of explanations. Individual failings included inability to 'cope' and violent temper. Environmental causes included poor housing, poverty and unemployment.

Table 4.3 Health visitors' views on causes of child abuse

	London HVs (n = 28)	*County HVs* (n = 20)
Cycle of deprivation	18	10
Individual failings	12	9
Environmental causes	13	6
Mothers' poor understanding of children's needs	8	6
Poor social network	5	3

Note: Many health visitors gave more than one cause.

Only one London health visitor believed that health visitors should have *no* part to play in child abuse, although, as an employee, she *had* to play a part. Three other health visitors (two London and one county) also expressed strongly the view that the monitoring role placed on them was an unpleasant one. They believed that the 'policing' aspect was detrimental to their role as professional friend. All the others accepted this function, with many echoing the view expressed by the Health Visitors' Association (*see* HVA, 1987a, page 11, para 1.24 and HVA 1987b introduction) that health visitors are well placed to identify and detect the first signs of abuse.

(Both health visitors are talking about their role in child abuse.)
'You have access to a family as a routine, provided they accept that of

course, but we are seeing them in an everyday capacity and I think in an ideal position to pick up when something in a normal situation becomes abnormal or potentially dangerous.'

HV: 'I mean the baby is born and the midwife comes in and then after 10 days the health visitor goes in. Well that's a very early stage in the set-up of a family with under-5s. That is the earliest contact you have and then you are constantly on the alert as to how the family is getting on, using the loose term how they are getting on. I suppose we all have a sort of a norm for any particular family that we would expect them to follow and indeed any deviation from that one would be aware of not just in the home, but when you meet them out or when they come to the clinic and maybe see another health visitor, we will always discuss each other's families that have attended.'

It is interesting to note how very few sample health visitors queried the appropriateness of this role. Two recent documents (Health Visitors' Association, 1987a,b) also suggest that health visitors generally do not question whether it is desirable and useful for health visitors to do this work. However, there are serious questions to be discussed among those who provide and plan welfare services.

Recent events (notably Cleveland) have highlighted the difficulties involved in identifying abuse and in the division of labour between workers. What constitutes child abuse is problematic, changes with time and is socially constructed; for example in Sweden it is illegal to hit a child, whereas public schools in England continue to regard this as a useful and legitimate means of disciplining children. Judgements about what constitutes child abuse are difficult to make. Criteria used to determine whether a case of child abuse has occurred are influenced by the beliefs, prejudices and values of workers (*see* for example Dingwall *et al.*, 1983). Health visitors are in danger of being lumbered with something which they cannot do. We need therefore to consider whether and how far this is an appropriate task for them.

First, is it feasible for health visitors in practice to detect child abuse by a system of routine home visiting? Many health visitors are simply unable to visit, because of their heavy caseloads. Even if they were able to visit routinely, how often would they have to visit to be sure of preventing and detecting child abuse? Secondly, it is important to ask whether it is desirable for the health worker who is employed as 'mother's friend', to act as 'policer' of households. Thirdly, do health visitors have any special skills (more than the rest of us) to prevent and detect child abuse?

SUMMARY AND DISCUSSION

To summarize the main issues raised here, mothers in our sample accepted the intervention of health visitors in the privacy of their homes mainly because they saw it as useful to prevent and identify child abuse, although they recognized and mostly appreciated the support and information-giving functions of health visitors, especially in the early days.

Although health visitors saw the prevention of child abuse as a very important aspect of their work, they stressed that their main task was educating mothers. They believed on the whole that they had expert factual knowledge about child-care and that mothers needed to be instructed in 'good' child-care methods. They routinely introduced certain topics, depending on the age of the child. Mothers on the other hand, appreciated access to health care workers but wished to have a service which responded to topics identified by them and not by the workers.

We have suggested that from the views of both mothers and health visitors, health visitors had two major functions, that of inspecting households for child abuse and that of health educator. But the fact that the health visitor has both these roles, makes her work difficult. As an employee in the health service she is both powerful and powerless. She is powerful in that she has a legitimate right to intervene in child-rearing and is in the position officially to label mothers as 'good' or 'bad'. In extreme conditions she also has access to coercive sanctions against parents. She is powerless in that, although increasingly held to account by society in cases of child abuse, she is not given the right of entry to the home. She needs to negotiate access to conduct both her policing and educative roles. In both cases, she needs the cooperation of mothers. She is a 'family visitor' but she has very little influence on fathers (*see* Chapter 3). She reaches the 'family' through the mother. Yet fathers may be influential in determining child health care, may have an active role in child-care, and are the main perpetrators of child abuse – as commonly defined.

As a health educator she faces certain difficulties. First, many health visitors believed they could change people's behaviour within a 'good relationship'. But such relationships may not exist. Many health visitors, especially in London, said they had insufficient time to visit and meet mothers. Some mothers are unwilling to allow any relationship to develop between themselves and health staff. Even those mothers who felt that they had a 'good relationship' with their health visitors, would nevertheless turn to other sources of inform-ation, such as friends, relatives, neighbours and the media. High mobility among both health visitors and parents of young children makes continuity of relationships difficult. One-quarter of the health visitors (in both samples) had been in the post for less than 3 years, and another quarter for less than 5. Mobility among parents was also high, as we found when seeking our sample (*see* Appendix 1). Of those interviewed (screening interview) one-quarter had lived in the district for less than 5 years.

Secondly, if we wish people to change their behaviour, a necessary condition is that they should be actively, positively and willingly engaged in an educational process (c.f. Strehlow, 1983). Health education is unlikely to be effective otherwise. Therefore health educators need to reconsider the appropriateness of a 'subtle' approach.

Thirdly, changing behaviour is itself a difficult task. Health educators are often asking people to make profound changes to their ways of life. This is no light matter. It becomes even more difficult and complex to ask people to do so on behalf of their children – so highly prized and such an important responsibility. It becomes even more crucial for people to be active and conscious participants in the education process.

Finally, we raise for discussion the question whether health visiting is and should be seen more as teaching or as social work (c.f. Sachs, 1988). In the last chapter we discuss the conflict health visitors and social workers face – between supporting people within their socioeconomic circumstances, and working with them to change those circumstances. In this chapter we have shown that health education is seen by health visitors as a major part of their work. Can they *do* both?

DISCUSSION TOPICS

1 Is it possible and desirable for the same person to work as both the 'policer' and the 'friendly adviser' of mothers?
2 What goals and methods of health education aimed at parents are appropriate?
3 Is the health visitor more like a teacher or more like a social worker?

FURTHER READING

On the education of mothers:
David, M. (1985). Motherhood and social policy – a matter of education? *Critical Social Policy*, **12**, 28–43.
On education:
Freire, P. (1972). *Pedagogy of the Oppressed*. Harmondsworth, Middx: Penguin.
On child abuse:
Dingwall, R., Eekelaar, J. and Murray, T. (1983). *The Protection of Children: State Intervention and Family Life*. Oxford: Blackwell.

CHAPTER 5
PERSPECTIVES ON CHILD HEALTH SERVICES

We saw in the last chapter how as child's advocate, the health visitor is concerned not only in ensuring the physical safety of the child, but also in educating mothers, with the aim of encouraging the development of the child's full potential. We consider here the evidence from our data on some aspects of the child health services: home visiting by health visitors, developmental assessments and immunization. We continue to explore some themes raised in the previous chapter: how far is the principle of universalistic surveillance shared by parents and by health workers, and how far do services that are provided for the whole child population meet the needs of individual parents? So an underlying running theme in this chapter is: how appropriate and how good are child health preventive services? As in other chapters, we give mothers' perspectives and then those of health visitors.

MOTHERS' PERSPECTIVES

Home visits and the value of health visitors

Mothers perceived the health visitor as concerned with the well-being of children, rather than adults. They believed health visitors came to their homes mainly to ensure that children were not being ill treated and that mothers were managing adequately as mothers. Even those who highlighted the benevolent side, mentioned the controlling and 'policing' element.

(This parent is answering the question, 'What do you think is the health visitor's role?')

'I would say firstly to assist parents, particularly new parents who have no experience in just making them realize that there is help at hand if needs be and that this information is available, and advice, first of all just health – what to do in this situation and then secondly health issues of how do you bring up a healthy child and what do you do when they, say, have growth problems. And then I'd say finally as watchdog you know to safeguard the children if you know there is danger of abuse or maltreatment or whatever just to pick that up if it is happening.'

An important point to make here is that although mothers accepted the principle of surveillance, this did not mean they accepted the unannounced visit (*see* also McIntosh, 1987). Health visitors talked of 'dropping in' and 'popping in'; these visits looked to many mothers more like inspection of their child-care standards. However, mothers also stressed the benevolent side of the health visitor's work.

I: 'What do you think is the health visitor's role?'
M: 'Help with kids, really, information, if you have any trouble you can go to them, ask questions and then they'll discuss it, tell you what's what.'

Many mothers, like the one just quoted, saw the health visitor as offering help. Help could include a variety of things such as information about the locality, the services available and advice on child-care. While health visitors talked of education as an important function of the home visit, mothers viewed it as an opportunity to ask for any help they might require. They believed in a parent-led service, with health workers responding to them. They would call the health visitor if they believed it was necessary, and they highly valued being able to do so. As this mother points out:

M: 'I haven't really had any problems you know, that I can – she's very nice, I think if you did have a bad problem she'd help you. She's caring and she listens.'

The potential helpfulness of health visitors was particularly important in two situations; first, in the early weeks following the birth of a child, and secondly for those mothers who lacked adequate social contacts.

Most of the mothers had highly valued the health visiting services when their child was born. However, at the time of our interviews, more saw the health visitor as rather a marginal figure in helping and advising them with child-care (Table 5.1).

Table 5.1 Mothers' views of health visitors' helpfulness

	Yes	No	Unsure	No help needed	HV not seen therefore cannot comment
HV helpful when child was a baby	21	6	1	5	
HV helpful *now* (child aged almost. 2 years)	8	7	—	12	6

n of mothers = 33

(This mother is talking about people she would contact if she was concerned about her child, now aged almost 2.)
I: 'What about your HV?'
M: 'In a way she doesn't come into the scene at all, because when they get to a certain age you don't have dealings with them, I mean you don't get in touch with them as a matter of course, you don't go.'

For those who lacked good social networks, health visitors had been very helpful; especially for the women who were new to this country and did not have significant (usually female) relatives here. Help in these cases had often included practical aspects of child-care. These mothers told us appreciatively how the health visitor had showed them how to care for their babies: bathing, feeding, sterilizing equipment, and that the health visiting service was especially important because they had no family here to consult.

(This mother is talking about writing to her own mother who lives abroad.)
'I write to my mum, but if I have a problem with him I don't want to worry her. Because she is the type of person who worries a lot so I try to keep it. She's a long way. If I had a problem she would catch the next flight. The person I turn to is my doctor and my health visitor.'

Mothers varied in which aspects of the health visitor's role they welcomed. Many had liked the fact that they could discuss wide ranging topics with her (12 mothers), others had valued advice given on child-care topics (10 mothers), and on health topics (eight mothers). About one-fifth of the mothers (six) appreciated the health visitor helping with day-care provisions and advising about welfare rights. Many mothers (17) noted appreciatively the friendliness of the health visitor and that she listened to what they had to say. They felt in return able to talk to her (15 mothers).

The health visiting service had, therefore, been very helpful to mothers in the early days of having a child. This was particularly the case for those who did not have the support of relatives and friends. Mothers now (first child aged nearly 2) no longer required this service so much because they now possessed both experience and knowledge. It remained, nevertheless, a potentially useful one. However, mothers believed *they* should initiate seeking help and advice from health workers. They perceived the home visit as surveillance for child abuse, but also as benevolence. That is, it gave them space to discuss topics of interest to them, and to seek help if they needed it.

Child health clinics

Mothers expressed similar views to those they made about home visiting when discussing child health clinics. They saw it as offering a parent-oriented service. They could seek advice there when *they* identified a need. The clinic was where they went to discuss an issue with health workers. Mothers (18) highly valued this access to health workers.

> (These mothers are talking about the value of clinics.)
> 'I was worried about Jenny's weight, so I was glad of the chance to go to chat, it was helpful.'
> 'The help was there and they used to ask you if you needed help so I was always sure I could get help whenever I wanted it.'

Here again, mothers felt less need to attend or consult health workers as their child became older. Either they felt confident about their own knowledge (*see also* Mayall, 1986), or they had access to other sources of advice. As Graham (1979a) notes, mothers attend clinic if they see it as meeting a need which cannot be satisfied elsewhere. It was especially important, therefore, for those mothers who had no, or poor, social support. Those mothers who were still attending clinic regularly, were likely to be the ones with no immediate family or friends to help, lonely mothers (*see* Mayall, 1986), and those who were relatively new to this country. For these mothers the clinic was an extremely important place, and for a few the *only place* they knew to obtain information or advice on any topic.

It is important for service providers and planners who wish to improve uptake of their services to take account of two important criticisms by parents of child health clinics which recur in research studies over the years. Both concern parental time. Both long waiting times and restricted opening hours are serious deterrents – the second especially so for parents in paid work.

(Here mothers are talking about their local clinics.)
M: 'The only thing that I feel is really wrong about the place is that you can sit round there for about 2½ hours which is – it's disgusting. I mean you imagine . . . you have to keep a baby amused for 2½ hours. She's not so bad now because she's running around, so she plays with all the toys now, but when you've got them little babies and they scream they're in there for so long. It's very badly organized, I mean she gets tired and by the time she gets in she's so irritable she'll scream and shout. When you first go round, you're not prepared for it. They (mothers) come in, they've got no feeds, no nappies and they have to get up and go.'
M: 'It's convenient for mothers who are not working. Mothers who are working don't really have the opportunity to go there, so I think that it would be a good thing if they opened one evening a week, 6.30–7.30 hours, so mothers who are working have a chance to go and chat about their children and their development.'

There seemed to be no doubt that all mothers valued the existence of child-health clinics. Health workers at the clinic were an extremely important resource. Indeed, the clinic was a valuable resource centre, a 'clearing house' for health topics and child-care issues, and for social matters such as housing and day-care. So it seems that open access and ease of access are therefore crucial. Access could be improved, especially for two groups of people – parents in paid employment, and those without social support who want a friendly place and an opportunity to meet people. This second group includes relative newcomers to this country. In their case, difficulty of access can be compounded by language difficulties and an unfriendly atmosphere. We shall return to the problems faced by this group in Chapter 7.

Developmental checks

Developmental checks are an established feature of services but their value is debatable. Currently an inter-professional working group is considering the factors worth screening (Hall, 1989). Here we are concerned with the service as presently offered and used. Service-providers and especially managers are concerned about the low or delayed take-up of developmental checks, especially the later ones. Mothers' perspectives are helpful in suggesting reasons for this: it was very important for them to establish the normalcy of the child. The majority of mothers (23) said that developmental assessments were performed to ensure that their child was developing normally, while others (8) talked in terms of detecting abnormalities. However, as their children grew older, they also became more confident (and did not need to consult professionals to reaffirm this point) that their child *was* developing normally. An extreme example of this confidence is the mother of the one child seen only for the 6-week check; the mother said that, as she was sure he was growing normally, he did not need to be seen. Though most children in the sample had had all the recommended checks so far (6 weeks, 8 months, 18 months), one may expect that take-up of later checks would tail off, as indeed nationally they do. Some mothers said that, because earlier checks had suggested their children were developing normally and they were also confident about their own assessment, they were now simply conforming to what health workers expected of them.

'Why did we have it done? Because it was there! Just because it's the system, you know and seeing they do them, you think well we may as well get them done. It certainly gives one a sense of security having it done.'

Although about half of the mothers (17) liked the assessments because 'it puts your mind at ease', they also said that they had not learned anything new about their child. They already knew their children were developing normally and it was simply reassuring that a professional had affirmed this.

Compliance was therefore an important reason for attending later developmental assessments. A few people also complied because they believed there was a policing element attached to developmental checks. For instance:

I: 'Why do you think they offer these checks, why do they ask parents to come?'
M: 'Oh that's a tricky one, I suppose to make sure the mothers are looking after their kids well, one thing that goes through my mind a lot why they do it, it's because of this child violence going around . . . but I'm really glad they do these check ups, they should do it.'

A few mothers, like this next one, a highly educated woman in a 'professional' occupation, believed there was an element of compulsion.

> 'I always kind of felt like they're absolutely compulsory. I'm not really sure what the position is on that, but you get a little card that tells you to go and you assume you have to go, or someone is going to be chasing you round. So I just went.'

Another important point for service providers and health workers to consider is that one-quarter of the mothers said that developmental checks were badly done. The examination was cursory, or the 'tests' were not very good.

> *M*: 'A doctor can't really say, take a child in a room for about 5 minutes and say a child is this or that. You can't in the space of 5 minutes.'
> *F*: 'It seems such a superficial kind of check. It depends entirely on the mood of the child at that point in time, whereas a real check would have a bunch of kids playing in a room, I think, with the doctor observing them for half an hour or something. You'd probably pick up more about the child than walking into a consulting room and putting four blocks on top of each other' (laughing).

A third important theme concerns the uneasiness of some mothers about developmental assessments. A number of mothers were worried that their child would not perform; they talked in terms of 'tests' which their children had to 'pass'. Some expressed concern that health workers had the power to label their child as not doing well while they themselves were sure that their child was developing normally.

> (This mother is talking about developmental assessments.)
> 'I know it was time for her to go . . . I was not really interested to go, because I mean they are going to assess my child and probably say she's not this, she's not that and I know what she is capable of, because I mean nobody knows the child but the mother.'

A few mothers had been caused anxiety when a diagnosis was made that turned out to be false (*see* quotation and comment Chapter 6, pp 112–113). The fact that records were kept by health workers and not made available to parents added a sinister touch:

> *M*: 'They told Aisha to build some bricks and she did not do it and probably they write down that she's not capable and things like that and at home she's able to do it.'

They felt that they should have access to records. One mother had asked the doctor what she was writing but this request was completely ignored. As she said, 'It would be nice to know what she wrote down. I mean wouldn't you like to know what doctors write about your child?'

Another mother wished health workers would contribute to the 'baby book' which she had been given at the clinic, for this was the record she kept about her child. 'I think they could, like in my book they've got a little space for notes, they never put notes in the book you know, to tell you anything – or after a check.'

To summarize mothers' views, although they believed that establishing normalcy was important, developmental checks were only one means of doing so. Earlier checks, their own knowledge and observations, talking to friends, and comparing their children with others, enabled them to judge whether or not their child was developing normally. They also held strong views about the quality of the test procedures carried out. These are two pointers to why take-up of developmental assessments declines as children grow older.

Immunization

Service-orientation to immunization presents a model of how services in general could be offered. We found that by and large both health workers and parents knew what their own and the others' responsibilities were, and agreed with each other. Discussions and decisions proceeded in the light of this basis of shared knowledge and agreement. We had a strong impression from our data that the workers' position on immunization had been more carefully worked out and agreed than for other child-care topics: health workers had knowledge which they sought to keep up-dated; they gave parents information on the subject; and the final decision was the parents' responsibility.

For most of the mothers in our sample the decision to have their child immunized had not been a problem. They knew the benefits and were determined that their children should be immunized.

I: 'How did you decide?'
M: 'There was nothing to decide, I just knew I wanted them done.'

Knowledge about immunization came from a variety of sources, relatives, friends, leaflets, magazines and the media. Most mothers

(22) reported discussion with health workers, mainly health visitors but also clinical medical officers, GPs, hospital doctors, medical friends and homeopaths. Mother arrived at a decision usually by consulting different people and drawing on various sources of information.

For some parents (9), however, the decision about the pertussis component had been a difficult one. Discussions with health workers led to different outcomes. Some remained adamant that their children should not be given the immunization; others accepted the arguments presented to them, and took the decision for immunization. As with other child-health topics, they appreciated the opportunity to explore the issue in partnership with health workers.

(This mother is describing a discussion on immunization with health workers.)
'It was shared (with the clinical medical officer and the health visitor) in a way I think, I actually made the decision in the end – yes I mean I was not pushed to do it but I got help as well about it.'

Once again, it was notably parents in paid employment who reported difficulties in having immunization carried out. Access to immunization sessions could be problematic, and this might affect take-up.

I: 'Did you have any difficulties having them (immunizations) done?'
M: 'When I started working it was difficult; the first injection was easy because I was not working. The second injection was semi-O.K. The third . . . oh it was hell. I think it took me about five times to come to the clinic. Because of the fact of getting time off work.'

To summarize mothers' perspectives on child-health services, mothers believed that services should be responsive to their needs. They strongly believed that these should be parent-led. They had no doubt that the responsibility for their children's health was primarily theirs. They valued access to health workers and exchange of information. They viewed unsolicited services such as the home visit primarily as policing, but they accepted this. The benevolent side of child health services was apparent when they had asked for help and received it. Their views also suggest reasons for non-uptake of services such as inadequate opening times.

Friendly, courteous, helpful and sensitive staff were very import-ant to mothers as users of child health services. They did not always encounter such staff. About one-half of the mothers expressed overt and in some cases strong negative comments about *a* health visitor, not necessarily their present one but a health visitor they had encountered. Negative points included: an unpleasant, patronizing or judgemental manner and the belittling of problems perceived by mothers. About one-quarter of the mothers (9) had found the health visitor unable or unwilling to offer assistance with help they had sought. This ranged from advice about breast-feeding to help with rehousing. A few (3) mentioned that health visitors were unable to offer anything constructive, about any issues of concern to them.

HEALTH VISITORS' PERSPECTIVES

Home visits

We continue to explore the two themes of child surveillance and benevolent service to mothers. In both London and county areas health visitors were required to carry out home visiting. Some health visitors did home visits because it was a task imposed on them, while others (the majority) believed it to be a good way of working. Employers expected them to visit households with young children, and 'routine' visiting was the ideal. The county health visitors, on the whole, could fulfil this ideal.

> (County health visitor talking about her visiting pattern.)
> *HV*: 'We visit for 5 weeks every week and they come to clinic for the 6 week check, . . . then we visit again at 3 months and the purpose of that visit is to give them some sort of food and guide them on to the right types of food not to encourage them to give it at 3 months but so that they start at 4 or even 5 months if they can . . . and then we visit again at 6 months and they have developmental assessment at 8 months and hearing test and then they would be seen again at a year by us in the home and then 18 months they would come for the developmental assessment – either they would be invited or we would go and visit to invite them if we can't get in touch with them any other way. And then we see them at 2 at home and then 3 at home and then they would have a developmental assessment again at 3 with an eye test. In our practice we do a urine test at 3 on all the 3 year olds, and 4½ – when they have pre-school booster we measure and weigh them then and ask the mothers if there is any worry at school.'

As discussed in Chapter 4, health workers felt intervention was necessary because they needed to oversee the difficult task of child rearing and to assess standards of care given by mothers.

Health visitors justified the 'routine' and universalistic pattern of working to cover all households because as one health visitor said:

'Let's put it this way, people would survive without it (HV service), but you are trying to elevate people, you are working towards the ideal.'

On this basis therefore every mother qualifies for the service of the health visitor, and every mother should be monitored.

I: 'What is it that you can contribute (to a household selected randomly by us) that no one else can?'
HV: 'Very little. She's a well educated, well read lady. Sometimes that's a problem for me – keeping up with ladies like that, very little other than routine monitoring. You can't assume that because someone is a speech therapist . . . they can be blind to their own children's areas of delay. So it's just routine.'

However, some health visitors, especially in London, were unable to carry out routine, universal visiting (*see* Table 4.1 p.66.). This next health visitor illustrates the views of many who discussed selective visiting. In practice they could not provide a universal service and, even more important, mothers might not require their services.

HV: 'I have rather mixed feelings about routine home visits because we are hard pushed to follow the guidelines . . . they are unrealistic in terms of numbers of families that we service. I am more inclined to say to people, if you have a problem and you would like a discussion, contact me rather than saying you must visit in a fortnight and then another fortnight because I feel that there is an enormous variation and people are very capable – if they have several children, they don't need you. They feel almost obliged to justify your appearance by thinking up things to make you feel good and their problems about this and that.'

A few health visitors illustrated their lack of autonomy and the constraint imposed on them. As employees they were required to carry out home visits, whether they wanted to or not.

I: 'How do you feel about offering your services, arriving on a doorstep and saying, "I'm your health visitor?"'
HV: 'Sometimes I feel a bit daunted and if you are feeling a bit fed up, it's quite hard to actually sell yourself because you think heavens I am sure they don't really want to see me especially if you don't want to see them! It is quite hard, you do get used to it, but often I think – heavens

they don't, I am sure, want to see me . . . it is quite hard actually to go and sometimes you wonder if you are going for yourself to ease your conscience.'

When asked a direct question about the purpose of the home visit, health visitors talked in terms of 'family surveillance', and 'assessing family dynamics' or evaluating the standard of care received by children.

> *I*: 'Do you think that home visiting is important and why?'
> *HV*: 'Oh yes, I think yes, well you can see them in their own homes and all the problems, you see the children and . . . behaving properly, you see the toys they have, you see generally you know how mums are, caring for the child and how they react at home.'

Surveillance, therefore, was an important aspect of home visiting. Recall that mothers also saw surveillance and policing as the main function of the home visit.

For mothers, the benevolent aspect of this service was that health visitors listened and responded to their requests for help. But for health visitors, the home visit was the setting for carrying out health education and attempting to change the behaviour of mothers. So there was a fundamental difference in perspective between the two parties.

Health visitors argued that in the home visit, mothers were more relaxed and could more easily raise topics. This was because they believed that mothers were in charge at home and felt able to discuss in the privacy of their homes, topics they would not raise in the clinic. The health visitor was also able to give more time to the meeting than at the clinic. We need to remember, however (*see* Chapter 4), that health visitors consistently told us that they had an agenda (often a hidden one) of topics they systematically introduced during the home visit, suggesting they controlled the encounter and were less responsive to topics mothers wished to discuss. Very few health visitors (4) queried the effectiveness of health education in this setting. Here is one:

> *I*: 'Do you think that parents value home visits?'
> *HV*: 'It depends what sort of visiting you are talking about. I mean if there is a crisis, if there is a problem and if it's a problem that the mother's brought to you, she will be interested in obtaining your help with that problem, yes. But from routine visiting, I think it's question-able as to what amount the mothers feel they are getting out of it, I'm

sure. I mean, you may go and visit one mother one day and be armed with lots of wonderful information . . . I don't know, hearing, when the mother is worried about the child's hearing that day in which case the two of you will hit it off well and have a good conversation and she'll be very glad you came. But if you are sitting there with lots of answers on subjects she did not have a problem over or didn't feel that she particularly wanted to discuss, I mean if you want to sit there piping on about fluoride for the child's teeth and it was not something she thought about she may well feel that this is an intrusion.'

We noted earlier that mothers disliked unannounced visiting. Many health visitors suggested that visiting by appointment was a good way of working. Several county health visitors reported visiting mainly by appointment – partly because 'their' mothers would probably have objected to workers 'dropping in' unannounced. Visiting by appointment removed some of the intrusive element of the visit and was also more conducive to effective health education, because mothers could assemble topics for discussion. These health visitors were recognizing the mothers' perspectives and priorities.

I: 'Do you think that home visits are important and why?'
HV: 'Well I do encourage people to come to me (at clinic) . . . and also if I do visit, I visit by appointment because I feel that it's an invasion of privacy just to turn up and rap on the door and I know I would not like it so I don't think that my clients do. Visiting by appointment gives them forewarning: they can store . . . you can often go in and there's a shopping list that they have drawn up, "by the way can I ask you this and this", whereas if you catch them unawares they don't make the most of that session.'

In sum, then, health visitors and mothers agreed on the surveillance function of home visiting. They had different perspectives on the benevolent side of this task. Mothers saw the home visit as a setting where health visitors could respond to their requests for help, health visitors saw it as a means of educating mothers.

Child health clinics

When we asked health visitors about the value of clinic sessions, most of them replied about the value to *them*. They talked in terms of value to parents only when prompted. About one-third of both samples of health visitors (10 London, 6 County) saw clinics as a means for health staff to monitor the health and the well-being of children. For other health visitors, clinic sessions were an efficient use of their time. Generally health visitors believed that mothers should use clinics and health services simply because they were there. Mothers should bring their children to be monitored by the health service, irrespective of their own perspectives on the need for their children to be seen. Recall that mothers' whole point was that it was up to them to decide when to go and that they also had their own agenda to discuss with health workers. They did not go to the clinic to be inspected!

In answer to our direct question about the value of clinics to parents some health visitors (10 London, 5 county) agreed with the mothers' view: it was valuable because parents could initiate use of services when they perceived a need.

Several health visitors (9 London, 9 county) saw the clinic as a meeting point for mothers. This is not a view shared by many mothers (*see also* Mayall, 1986). In this study, many of the women from ethnic minorities had experienced difficulties making social contact with white British mothers. They talked of the unfriendly British, of their inability to make contact with the indigenous population and gave graphic accounts of their sense of loneliness in the midst of British mothers, a point we take up again in Chapter 7.

A few health visitors and clinical medical officers criticized the quality of clinics, especially the long waiting times and unpleasant surroundings.

Developmental checks

For health visitors, as for mothers, these were mainly to assess normalcy. Clinical medical officers also talked in terms of assessing normalcy. However, while mothers believed that after a time their children's development probably did not need to be checked, health workers believed that children should continually be assessed over the years. Some health visitors (13 London, 8 county) saw developmental assessment as child surveillance, as a means of 'keeping an eye' on the whole child population. Very few health visitors queried the need to continue assessing children. Those who did (4 London, 2 county) believed that parents were usually the ones to identify problems and to bring them to the attention of health workers.

Compared to the mothers, few health visitors (6, all from London) criticized the quality of developmental checks; these also talked of the long waiting time. Clinical medical officers commented that it was difficult to give a good service when there were long queues of people waiting to see them.

Mothers' concern that staff recorded views on their child which were then kept at the clinics was not echoed by health workers. Neither health visitors nor clinical medical officers talked about ownership of clinic records as in any way problematic.

Immunization

As we said earlier, there was most agreement between mothers and health workers on the subject of immunization. It stands out as a topic to which health workers have given serious attention. For example, district health authorities have considered the role of health workers and have issued guidelines to their employees, and provided training sessions, while promoting uptake for all children residing in their locality for public health reasons.

About one-third of the health visitors in both samples (11 London, 6 county), viewed their role simply as that of providing information to parents and giving parents the opportunity to discuss the issue. This was the line taken also by most clinical medical officers.

> *I:* 'So what do you see as your role (re immunization)?'
> *HV:* 'Giving information and allowing them to make a decision and respecting that decision, and if they refuse it, they refuse it. I don't see any point in badgering them to have it, it's their decision . . . if I kept badgering, they're not going to and why should I? I've done my role . . . they're perfectly reasonable.'

These health workers agreed with mothers that decisions on immunization were entirely the responsibility of parents.

Most health visitors believed that their role was to *encourage* parents to have their children immunized (17 London, 14 county). The form this took however, varied from mild encouragement, to 'pushing' people to take up immunization, to 'chasing up defaulters'. It is interesting to note, however, that even health visitors who appeared to be prescriptive and authoritarian regarding other health topics (as discussed in the previous chapter) adopted a 'softer' style when discussing immunization. They accepted more readily that they should not 'push' parents to have their children immunized especially in respect of the controversial pertussis vaccine.

Three of the clinical medical officers also talked in terms of encouraging uptake. But they believed that the health visitor was the person whose task it was to persuade parents. The health visitor therefore had the difficult role of persuasion, while the doctor merely presented information and allowed parents to decide. The health visitor's role was interventionist, the doctor's merely responsive.

Several health visitors took the view that parents would not seek out immunization for their children unless health workers encouraged them.

> '. . . generally I think it's people in the minority that actively seek out immunization.'

This view was not shared by parents!

Others, however, recognized that most parents took their responsibility seriously. They also acknowledged that for many parents to decide whether or not to immunize a child using a controversial vaccine could be difficult.

> *HV*: 'When I first qualified as a health visitor I just used to sort of spout on, you know; "Our feeling is that you should have the whooping cough immunization". I mean that's the one that's controversial . . . Now I don't feel able to push either side, especially since I've had a child of my own. I mean I just state that figures are open to inter pretation, somebody brings one set of statistics, I'm sure you can find another. I mean the more programmes I see where they debate whooping cough vaccination, the more unsure I feel about discussing it with people so it's not something I enjoy at all.'

Only three health visitors talked explicitly in terms of having a public health role. These health visitors acknowledged possible conflicts: while they were concerned with the child population as a whole, parents were concerned for their own, particular, loved child (an important difference in perspective, discussed in Mayall, 1986.)

Before ending this section on health visitors' perspectives on the services, we need to point out that most health visitors and clinical medical officers suggested that the services generally were excellent. If they were not used mothers were to be blamed. The quality of the service was not an issue.

> *I*: 'You work in an area with some very wealthy and some very poor people. And nationally it looks as if children have unequal chances of health. How do you see your role/work in these circumstances?'

HV: 'Oh gosh, that's difficult isn't it . . . do I see it as a problem? I don't see it as a problem, although they have got it, but the thing is here we really offer a lot to the mothers and it's the mothers who don't take up the offers. Things like eyes, squints and hearing problems . . . and psychological problems, they are all referred and within weeks they get seen. It's the mothers who don't take it up, so it's nothing to do with unequal health care as such. Because the rich people will go and take their children, will keep appointments, while these people, working class people don't want to keep appointments. Of course, then we get the complaint that they've got unequal health care, but have they got unequal health care, I would say.'

Only a few emphasized that services should be critically scrutinized if mothers failed to use them.

HV: '. . . If the people don't use it (the service) you have got to look to your own morals and this well why don't they. Is it just because generally the set-up is too difficult to get into? – are your phone calls never answered? or do you always have to leave a message, are people rude to you on the phone? . . . I can't blame the people that don't use it.'

DISCUSSION

The home visit

To conclude this chapter we suggest some discussion issues on preventive child-health services. First, the home visit, especially the unsolicited one, is problematic. There are currently two conflicting aims, in the eyes of both health visitors and other service-providers: offering friendly advice and 'inspecting' households. This dilemma is as yet unresolved. For example, while a document (HVA, 1987a, page 29, para 3.10) strongly recommends that visits should take place by appointment – to remove the policing intrusive aspect – it also suggests that routine visiting must be continued as this task is 'necessary for the detection of developmental defects, deprivation or abuse' (page 23, para 3.5). Mothers perceive the home visit primarily as inspection. While health workers may think that mothers are more relaxed at home, mothers may disagree. Some feel obliged to allow health visitors into their homes, partly out of politeness and partly if they believe health workers have a legitimate role (and right of access) in policing households for child abuse. They may fear the consequences of refusing access to these workers. Since the unannounced visit is seen by mothers primarily as judging their standards of mothering, it may be questioned whether it is a good setting for education. On the other hand, if mothers ask for the visit, then it may provide a setting for a discussion, useful to the mother, of topics raised by her.

Secondly, even if the home visit is considered to be desirable, health visitors need to discuss the feasibility of universalist home visiting. The health visiting profession remains committed to universalist home visits. It is reluctant to endorse selective visiting because those visited may be stigmatized (*see* for example, HVA, 1987a, page 29, para 3.11). But while in theory the service is universalist, in practice it may not be. It appears that health visitors do offer a universalist service to young babies, but their pattern of visiting becomes selective as the child grows older.

In the London area, according to the health visitor official returns, few children aged 1–5 seem to be visited when compared to those under the age of one. Mayall (1986) found that over a half of mothers in classes IV and V had been visited in the last 3 months, compared with a quarter of other mothers. Moss *et al*. (1986) have documented how visits decline over the child's first year. Half of the mothers in their study were visited between the ages of 7 weeks and 6 months and a third between the ages of 6 months and one year, although they had all been visited regularly in the first 6 weeks. In our sample, health visitors had to set priorities. Those who could not call on all the households in their caseload (as was especially the case in London) visited all newborn babies and the households they perceived to be problematic. Harrison (1986) has documented how health visitors offer a service of 'priorities within priorities' especially during staff shortage.

Clinic-based services

Next we raise some issues about clinic-based services. First some points about child surveillance and screening. We all accept and welcome the monitoring of children's health and development by people with training. As noted earlier, we need continuously to assess which 'checks' it is crucial for children to have (Hall, 1989), and if we want high take-up, we should make information on their purposes and value available to both paid and unpaid health care workers.

Secondly, a more flexible approach to screening children might be more appropriate. An interesting example is that proposed by Nicoll (1983). He suggests that workers should assess the few minimal checks which ideally all children should have. Their aim then would be to offer these to all children, but generally services would be flexible with children being referred by parents and by health workers as and when necessary.

Thirdly, we think it is important to provide adequate information to parents. We explained earlier how health workers have responded to public demand for more information and discussion on the topic of immunization. The views of mothers were more attuned to those of health workers on the subject of immunization than on that of developmental assessments. Better informed discussion between the two sides might lead to better understanding and take-up of developmental assessments. For example, parents could be given written information on why it matters that their children should receive an 18-months developmental assessment.

Fourthly, some providers, especially managers, need to give serious consideration to the quality of services they offer. It has become a commonplace finding that people note they have to wait at clinics. The fact that this is common should not lead us to assume that it is acceptable. People's non-use of services might be due to poor quality.

We have noted that some women find English people unfriendly and that some, especially newcomers, lack enough friends. Clinics could perhaps help here, by working towards enabling those who wish to meet people and form friendships to do so. It would seem, on our evidence, that servicestaff would have to do more than open their doors. They would have to take positive steps to bring people together.

Finally, we noted earlier that there was unease from mothers about the availability of records and about who owns the information gathered by health workers about their child. Possibly health workers do not think this is an issue; but what is routine to doctors may look ominous to parents. The underlying attitude of doctors and other health workers suggests an unequal power relationship and assumptions about divisions of responsibility for child health. It suggests to parents that health workers feel they know better than the parents; they do not need to share information, and parents are not capable of understanding information. It implies a balance of responsibility in favour of health workers. Parents are requested, and expected, to bring their children for inspection. However, health workers reserve the right to 'hide' things from them. We note that in France, and Oxfordshire (Saffin, 1985), parents hold the main child health record. No ill effects have been recorded! Parents are pleased to have the book and the information it contains (Greene and MacFarlane, 1985). WHO (1985) has added its weight to the arguments: they note that the best way to guarantee the availability of the health record to all services is for it to be home based.

ISSUES FOR DISCUSSION

1 Should usage of preventive child health services be the responsibility of parents or of health workers?
2 Who should keep child health records?
3 Do providers of health services need to reconsider the function of the traditional home visiting?
4 What is the appropriate division of responsibility between parents and others for child health care?

FURTHER READING

Armstrong D. (1983). *Political anatomy of the body – medical knowledge in Britain in the 20th century*. In *Provocative history of the child health services* Chapter 6. Cambridge: Cambridge University Press.
Nicoll A. (1983). Community child health services – for better or worse? *Health Visitor Journal*, 56 (7), 241–243.

CHAPTER 6
DIVISIONS OF LABOUR IN CHILD HEALTH CARE: PAID AND UNPAID WORKERS

In this chapter we explore mainly demarcations of role between *paid* workers – health visitors, doctors and social workers. We consider the nature of the cooperation and the relationships between these workers as well as looking at the tasks which are specific to them. While considering these varied roles in service provision, we think it is essential constantly to ask whether parents and children benefit from the division of labour which exists and what steps, if any, paid workers need to take to ensure maximal benefit to the unpaid people in child-care work, and their children.

In this context it is useful to raise here the issue of what is meant by 'providing services'. For example, to what extent do workers carve out areas of work which benefit their own occupational groups and to what extent do they consider what is entailed in serving people? The idea of a 'service' suggests that paid workers will respond to what people ask from them. Is this the case in child preventive health services? Or do workers provide the services they themselves consider to be appropriate and then expect mothers to use these? As we noted in the previous chapter, health workers tended to perceive child services as good or even excellent; it was clear that mothers should use them; and many health visitors thought encouraging uptake of services an important role. We have also noted that the services offered in child health are aimed at women; most of the workers are also women.

DIVISION OF LABOUR BETWEEN PAID WORKERS

Health visitors and doctors

Differentials in power and status seemed to affect both the quality of the working relationships and the demarcation of roles between workers. Clinical medical officers occupy a lower status in comparison with general practitioners. Most are women (all in our sample), often working part time in a branch of medicine which is assigned low status. However, *vis-à-vis* nurses such as health visitors, they occupy a higher rank in the hierarchy. This was reflected in the way they often talked in terms of the health visitors working not with them but *for* them, or working for a service with them (doctors) at the top.

Health visitors, however, played down differentials in power and status between themselves and clinical medical officers. The fact that these doctors were 'nice' people seemed to conceal from health visitors the doctors' perception of themselves as superior to health visitors.

Health visitors were more likely to perceive differential status between themselves and GPs. Some health visitors who met both GPs and clinical medical officers believed it was easier to achieve teamwork with clinical medical officers than with GPs. They suggested that the autonomy of GPs was a major hurdle. Not only did they have higher status, but they were also independent from health authorities closer teamwork with general practitioners would be difficult to achieve unless they became employees of health authorities.

In a clinic setting, both the health visitor and the clinical medical officer have clear functions established by tradition. The doctor has a limited technical role and the health visitor provides information and advice, with both workers seeing their work as complementary. However, in the case of the GP, the doctor is the established main worker 'in charge' of the surgery. The health visitor is brought in to help the doctor and her functions in a surgery setting are less clear than in a traditional clinic setting. It seemed from our data that clinical medical officers saw the importance of having a good working relationship with health visitors. General practitioners chose, or did not choose, to make an effort to work well with others. For instance, it was low on their list of priorities to attend team meetings.

(County health visitor talking about a team meeting.)

'. . . then there was a "communication needs within the primary health care team", a meeting of GPs, district nurses, health visitors, practice nurses, not many GPs there. Our lot (GPs at the practice where she works) were seeing their accountant (laughing). I shouldn't laugh but they are financially orientated, a lot of them. The others, there were two, three GPs, they did contribute but were we . . . the communication, it was to the converted, that come there and the ones that were missing are the ones that you need to encourage.'

Jefferys and Sachs (1983) note how women workers including nurses and health visitors accepted the unequal power relationship between themselves and general practitioners. Conflict was reduced if nurses accepted the doctors' authority in the group practice (Jefferys and Sachs, 1983, p. 233). Our health visitors also stressed trying to achieve good working relationships with doctors. The aim was to have a conflict-free working situation. We may ask, then, to what extent do health visitors accept a subordinate role in order to achieve this conflict-free situation?

To a large extent, satisfaction about working relationships with other workers depended on the individual characteristics and personalities of the people involved. Health visitors saw friendliness as an important characteristic in the doctors – it enabled them to work together. Notably, clinical medical officers did not see personal characteristics of HVs as contributing to a good working relationship. In other words, it was when doctors were nice and friendly that their superior status gave way to good personal relationships. Because the relationship was unequal this friendliness had to come from doctors; it was they who could make the unequal relationship easier and pleasanter.

However, a crucial ingredient of 'good' working relationships was that all types of workers understood and respected role demarcations. Some health visitors felt that confusions about the division of work were more likely to arise with GPs than with clinical medical officers. Health visitors felt frustrated if doctors did not understand their role.

(A health visitor who is GP-attached and based in a practice was very unhappy as she believed that the doctor did not understand her role. She is talking about a mother who repeatedly saw the GPs about child management; this she saw as her job. In this case the GPs were also annoyed at the recurrent visits of this mother to the surgery.)
HV: 'The GPs were getting a bit fed up with it and I was thinking, at first I thought, "I'll intervene", then I thought "No, let them get on with it" because if she is coming to do things about child management twice a

week and we're upstairs and they should know what we're about and they haven't bothered to, all they do is just grumble, grumble to the receptionist . . . I mean that was a splendid opportunity to say, "OK, let's call the health visitor down, you know and let's have a discussion, let's work out a strategy to cope with the situation", but they don't. That's just one very good example of how we don't communicate effectively with the GPs.'

There was a clear demarcation of roles between clinical medical officers and health visitors. Doctors dealt with physical health and provided a technical service. Health visitors dealt with the social and psychological aspects of health. Both sides accepted this division of expertise, knowledge and work patterns. The clinical medical officers said their role was to carry out medical examinations – skills which in this country are attributed to doctors and not to nurses. On the whole, their role was not to give advice, although some doctors had particular hobby-horses – topics they said they were keen to raise with mothers –'stimulation' and breast-feeding, for example. But in general, giving advice was the realm of the health visitor. Clinical medical officers would sometimes reinforce what the health visitor had said, but saw advice-giving as problematic.

(This clinical medical officer is talking about giving advice to parents.) 'I mean I think giving advice is really very difficult, I think one can't really give advice generally speaking. If you want to make a generalization I don't think one should go round giving advice because people aren't going to listen – I think it's a fallacy. I mean you give advice when – and if you're asked sometimes – you think people are asking for advice but they are not at all. And you think you're giving them advice and people just think you're talking a load of rubbish. So I mean one must be very realistic about giving advice and I think perhaps that is one of the problems with the health visitors in a way. Thinking about it, it's a very Victorian sort of charitable attitude perhaps saying well we're going to go out and dish out a bit of advice, I don't think it works, I think people have their own ideas, which they've got from various sources – books, friends and goodness knows what. Sometimes what they need to know is what is the current thinking or what advice out of all this stuff they've been given is correct and sometimes a doctor is quite important, or the doctor is put on a bit of a pedestal and they think your advice is quite good.'

The clinical medical officers viewed health visitors as workers who provided them with details of social background of families; and who also dealt with social problems which arose and encouraged parents to take up the services.

I: 'How do you see the health visitor's role in the preventive child health services?'

CMO: 'Well theirs is the most important role, I think. I mean we are a back-up to them, they do the new birth visit, pick up any problems as early as possible with the mother and the child and get help for them if needed, get them to the clinic if appropriate for checks and they are the ones that the mothers first turn to when they are worried when something goes wrong.'

I: 'And your role, you say you see it as a back-up, what do you mean by that?'

CMO: 'Well the health visitor gets them to me for these check ups and for problems. But she deals with the problem if she can first, she'll only bring them to us when extra help is needed.'

I: 'What do you see as being the health visitor's role?'

CMO: 'I think very much as the person who is right at the forefront, that has the initial contact with the children and with their parents. And presumably they will have notifications of the births, so they will be aware of all the children that ought to be followed up. Visiting the homes is obviously a really important thing that they do, starting right from the beginning, the visit after the birth and their contact with them, picking up any problems and encouraging them to come in initially for weighing but to make contact, to see them or the CMO if there are any problems or they feel that there are – I mean in an emotional sense or a physical sense. Or with the GP. I think that is just as important and I think more so. Encouraging them to come up for the immunizations and for the developmental checks. But I think really just to be the professional that is most close to actually what is happening.'

Health visitors agreed that their province was the social aspects of health. They also identified themselves as the health workers who gave mothers time for full discussion; doctors, especially GPs, did not provide that service.

I: 'What is it that you can contribute to their health that no one else can?'

(Health visitor is talking about a household we had chosen at random from her caseload.)

HV: 'I think probably, well I think other people could contribute but I think giving her the time to discuss the problems and time to listen to her and to try and talk through the things and advise her. I think, you know there's probably not that many people that can do that. I mean the doctor might be one of the people who could do that but most of them haven't got that sort of time to sit and discuss.'

So health visitors found that mothers came to them with problems that were important but which mothers felt they could not 'trouble' a doctor with.

Some health visitors argued in favour of GPs offering preventive child health services on the grounds that GPs knew the child as part of the family and so could therefore offer a better service. But in many cases – as reported both by 'group attached' health visitors and by parents – mothers did not necessarily see the GP with whom the child was registered. The common practice was for one or two partners interested in child health to offer such a service. So it seemed there was no guarantee in practice that the GP doing preventive work would be the one a mother saw for the curative side. We do not know how general this problem is.

An important distinguishing feature between health visitors and doctors was that while doctors offered a responsive service, health visitors were interventionist. Both clinical medical officers and GPs who offer child health preventive services work on a curative service model: they sit in clinics and wait for people to come to them. Health visitors seek out people and encourage them to use services.

It is interesting that some clinical medical officers appreciated – more clearly than most health visitors we interviewed – possible problems of an interventionist and unsolicited service.

I: 'You were talking about structures and staff. What do you see as being the health visitor's part in all this?'
CMO: 'Well, again you see I mean traditionally they've been, as we often joke at the clinic, the nosey parker who pops in, and I think there's a justification of that image. I mean I would go mad if some health visitor knocked on my door and I'd just had a baby and was slopping about and the place was filthy, and I think they do and I think a lot of them are quite judgemental, as lots of people are anyway. And I think probably one feels probably quite threatened by this person coming around being very efficient and everything, but I think that they can actually give a lot of help and advice and reassurance, which I think is very important. And particularly if there's no longer any support in your family and your mother isn't round the corner, the health visitor is very important.'

(Another clinical medical officer is talking of problems of an interventionist service. She refers to a mother (a 'girl') who came to clinic.)
CMO: 'I mean I think they don't like us knocking on the door – being nosey, asking questions. I mean this girl who was in tears yesterday: I don't want you finding out about my private life, just because I'm not married and all that stuff, and feeling very vulnerable, and I think that is one of the problems of the services – of the community – all these

people getting involved and you know, the worse mess you are in, the
more deprived you are, the more people come running round, trying to
help you but I don't think they do really. It's rubbing salt in the wound
and all that. So then you have to spill your heart out to the health visitor
and then the next day the social worker is knocking on the door, and
then the next day it's the police – I think it's terrible, so I think I'm sure
parents get absolutely mad about it, well I know they do, I mean I get
mad.'

It seems that health visitors and clinical medical officers agreed
about the division of labour between them. Doctors dealt with the
physical and health visitors with the psychological and social aspects
of health. Doctors offered a service in response to people's requests,
health visitors offered an interventionist service. Team work was
achieved by workers understanding and respecting each other's role.
The personalities and friendliness of individual workers also helped in
good teamwork. The independent status of GPs meant that power
relationships were unequal, but clinical medical officers also saw
themselves in a hierarchy where they were 'superior' to health
visitors.

Health visitors and social workers

Here we can suggest some points about health visitors' perceptions.
We do not have data from social workers. However, understandings
and misunderstandings may be common to both groups. Health
visitors saw themselves as primarily concerned with the health of
children, whereas social workers essentially worked on 'problems',
such as poor housing, violent households and child abuse; they also
had access to resources. But health visitors' and social workers' roles
overlapped more than those of health visitors and doctors' because
both kinds of workers were concerned with individuals in their social
context. Difficulties arose for health visitors when social workers
failed to understand the limits of the health visitor's role and expected
more than she could give.

As with doctors, therefore, good team work was achieved through
social workers' and health visitors' mutual understanding of their
work and working conditions.

I: 'What do you consider to be a reasonable caseload?'
HV: 'It depends on the area or the person.'

I: 'For you in this area?'

HV: 'I think I've got a reasonable caseload myself, if I'm always to concentrate on that, right? And not expected to be a bit of a social worker as well. And if the social worker understands the limitations of my job and does not off the top of her head think, oh she (i.e. the HV) has a duty to visit children under-5. I mean, they come up with funny ideas about how often we visit families – and things like that. And so do the schools and so does everybody else. How much we actually know about the families. If you only see a child once a year after the age of 2, you don't know a lot about them. But, you know if there is a problem, you can feel a bit of a fool. They say, "oh you're the one who actually visited that family, what did you discover? How were things in those days?" Well, it can be a bit hard-going – you say to them, "well, I'm not visiting 30, I'm visiting 200, they change all the time blah, blah . . ." It's difficult to get people to appreciate the tensions.'

The division of labour between health visitors and social workers in child abuse is the subject of much discussion (British Association of Social Workers and HVA, 1982; Laing, 1986); and there may be some conflict between the two sets of workers (Fawcett-Hennessy, 1986). Health visitors talked of the social worker as the main worker once a case of abuse had occurred. However, at times there was conflict. In some cases workers disagreed about whether or not a child was 'at risk'.

HV: 'At the moment I'm very concerned about the welfare of two children, one is aged 20–25 months now and the other little one is coming up for 4 months. And I'm particularly anxious about this family, but social services won't take them on because there is actually nothing, they have not been abused (laughing), they won't take them on. And they have not been allocated a social worker because they have not perceived the danger of the family and that I find very frustrating.'

In other cases health visitors believed that social workers had the wrong expectations about their role in child abuse which jeopardized what they felt to be their 'real' functions. This example illustrates the tension where the worker tries to be both friend and policer of a household.

HV: 'I feel that I have been under pressure to take on a much more policing of the family role by social workers and I think in most cases it has in fact damaged my relationship.'

I: 'Do you want to give an example?'

HV: 'Well, I've got two children on the abuse register and the family are having a lot of services. The children are 6 and educationally retarded; child of 6 and child of 2½ with lots of social work going into the family. The family are attending, mum and the little one are attending the family centre, and the others are attending a special school and in the summer holidays. I have been visiting up until then on a more regular basis than I would do, which in actual fact the mother wasn't pleased about. But during the summer holidays the situation broke down in which the family refused any social worker intervention and mum allowed me in again after I came back from my holidays, until I actually wanted to weigh and measure and she queried why her child should be weighed and measured when she knew that the children in the same road were not being weighed and measured; and subsequent to that I haven't been allowed in again. And so I felt that really I've had lots of pressure from social workers. They actually wanted me to go in three times a week, which certainly wasn't the healthiest thing; to go in to a child three times a week, to a child that is healthy and normal, and subsequently I've lost my access to the house completely, which I think is quite sad.'

Some health visitors tried to delineate their role *vis-à-vis* that of the social worker, but this was not easy as both types of worker dealt with the social aspects of health.

(This health visitor is talking about the five households on her caseload who are on the 'child abuse register' kept by social services.)
I: 'What is your job in these cases?'
HV: 'I usually make it known to them (the parents) that I know about it. I tell them if I've been to a case conference. I think they find out anyway, so you might as well be honest from the start. I think my job is to concentrate on the child's health and to within the family monitor the child's health, and to discuss health . . . social thing, I'm not a social worker.'
I: 'There is always a social worker?'
HV: 'There's always the social worker involved and that's always the key worker. It's very difficult because not only do the roles overlap but it's, you know, bad housing will affect their health, damp will affect their health. So you have to be aware of the social issues, but I think I've learnt it the hard way. If I can actually separate – I say, "I am the health visitor" and I say "I'm there to give the best help I can"; in that situation it makes my job easier. And it makes them clearer why I'm there. It's very difficult though.'

HV: 'Nobody seems to know how to define our responsibilities – the papers know how – they say – "ah she went in, she didn't notice the child, she's responsible". But then management say that you're not, that you're a health visitor, not a social worker. That doesn't hold water in court. So I think that what management need to do, what I would like to have seen done years ago is for them to face this aspect —of the job and to say, well if they are now taking in, being held responsible for all sorts of child abuse things . . . and if these girls are in fact in the front line of finding out how a child is cared for — which we are because we're the front line, it's no good saying any longer we're just there for health reasons. The two things aren't true. There's a bit of a line between them. Perhaps in the past it was, it could have been considered true. They weren't as aware, and they didn't have, because child abuse, non-accidental injury, is something which became documented from my reading when I started health visiting in the 1960s and people became aware of it then. But I think it's changed and that's changed our responsibilities in itself. 'Cos you're supposed to notice these things — and if you don't . . . But in the past you, one really was visiting because you were worried in case the kiddie was being badly treated; you were visiting more as an inspector, looking at the child, how it got the proper bedding and — totally different job we've got now.'

Paid and unpaid child health workers

It is inevitable that paid workers divide tasks, but there will be implications in that division of labour for people who use their services. For instance, what this division of labour means is that a parent might have to see a variety of people about one child. For an average child, in the first 5 years, a parent might need to see a GP, a health visitor, a clinical medical officer, a dentist and also possibly other workers such as hospital staff, speech therapist, social worker. Drawing on this collection of encounters about aspects of the child, the parent must derive the information he or she seeks to care for the whole child.

There may be difficulties for parents in this division of labour among paid workers. Paid workers may offer conflicting diagnoses, views and advice and parents may not know whom to consult. The first example also illustrates the difficult dilemma which health workers have: whether or not to share their worries and anxieties before a firm diagnosis can be made with parents.

(Mother talking about seeing the health visitor and the clinical medical officer at clinic initially because her baby had lost weight.)
M: 'I went into the health visitor and she said "the baby's a bit floppy, I'm worried, will you see the doctor?" (clinic doctor). So I went into the doctor and the doctor said, "your baby is not holding her head

properly. I'll write you a letter for your GP" and I was in a state, I was in a terrible state, I rang my mother and she was nearly sort of crying, "Oh my God what's the matter, we'll pay for a specialist" and everyone was really panicking like mad. And then I rang my husband's mother who's a great deal more practical than my own mother and she said "get rid of that bloody health visitor, they're poison, you know, don't let them into your house, they tell you a lot of old baloney, take no notice . . ." and I had Tom's sisters on the phone saying "get rid of those health visitors, they're terrible, they wind you up, they get you thinking all sorts of things that aren't true". And then I had people ringing in from work saying don't listen to anybody, just go to your doctor. And I went to my doctor and my doctor said, "I don't know what that woman is talking about, there's nothing the matter with her head". But I had been fretting, really fretting, that was really a tears job – you know, my child has got something terrible.'

I: 'Did you think it was possible there was something wrong with her?'
M: 'Oh yes.'
I: 'Did it alter your perception of her?'
M: 'Well, no, I don't think really. I mean I suppose I've had that kind of – whatever a doctor tells you must be true. At the clinic they kept telling me – "oh, she's got too much weight on for her height", when I took her the following week to the hospital (a London teaching hospital), they said "nothing like that, don't worry yourself about it", so I mean you sort of are in the middle of the road, aren't you?'

(Mother talking about her encounters at clinic with health visitor and clinic doctor – in this case the paid workers were worried about the child's weight, but the mother was not concerned because she knew that her child was eating very well and all members of both her own and her husband's families were very slim.)

I: 'What did you say when the doctor mentioned this subject?'
M: 'Well I didn't bother to ask her what she could do about it – because I thought to myself, she's talking a lot of rubbish. I'm not at all worried about him, so I just sort of said – well, OK, if he's not changed in 6 months I'll bring him back.'

M: 'About problems about where you live, it would be nice to have someone that could help you. You just don't know who to turn to, you end up ringing everyone and everyone rings you to advise you to ring everyone else. I thought that your social worker would be able to help you on problems like that but there you are.'

DISCUSSION

Division of responsibility between unpaid and paid workers

This account of the division of labour between paid and unpaid workers in child health care has raised the issue of responsibility. As the previous chapters have suggested, many health visitors viewed a large proportion of mothers as irresponsible. Part of the division of labour, therefore, was the need for paid health workers to encourage the unpaid mothers to do the right things for their children. We should say that we do not share this view. There is nothing in the data from this study to suggest that mothers are irresponsible people. Their orientation to child-care is, naturally, far more responsible than that of paid workers, in that they take it on for the whole long period of years that their children depend on them. Other studies (Graham, 1984; Mayall, 1986) and this present study have all concluded that mothers are very aware of the needs of children and act in very responsible ways. There are very few exceptions to this rule. Leaving aside research, it is obvious that they are the people who take the major, sometimes sole responsibility for their children over many years, and must radically change their way of life to do so. As Graham (1984) points out, it is important for health workers to be aware that mothers are not irresponsible, but often face 'conflict of responsibilities'; they have to reconcile how best to care for their children's health with the many other demands made on them. Indeed mothers (and some fathers) constantly have to compromise between priorities in health care. For example, a mother may put a sick or tired child to bed without washing her or- cleaning her teeth because she gives priority that evening to one set of health needs (the need for rest) over another (the need for hygiene). At times behaviour that may appear to be irresponsible to a professional eye is, paradoxically, responsible behaviour.

Furthermore, there are benefits if paid health workers recognize that mothers are indeed responsible. Mothers are relieved of harassment and blame from health workers and relationships may improve. Health workers are relieved of the burden of feeling *they* must take responsibility for child welfare and must harass mothers. Then they can devote more time to other community health work and use their skills in a more profitable and satisfying way.

It is important for those who work at the interface of people and services to make their own perspectives explicit and to think about links between behaviours and wider social structures. Otherwise they risk alienating those in greatest need of help and support. There may be dissonance between mothers' and paid workers' perspectives here which workers need to consider when discussing appropriate ways of delivering their services. In the UK, since child-care is not officially recognized as a kind of work meriting public recognition, there is little in the way of financial resource, practical help and social support which health and welfare workers can offer to mothers in their task of mothering (cf. David, 1985). Such workers may feel impelled to label mothers just because they cannot offer practical help. In the next chapter we shall continue to explore the dangers of individualizing problems while down-playing the influence of social structures and institutions which may create and maintain these problems.

As regards who does the work of child-care, there is, it seems, a danger that paid workers will overestimate their own contribution and underplay the work of the principal child-care workers – mothers, who by their work are actively involved in the production of health (Graham, 1979b; Cresson, 1986; Mayall, 1986). It is commonly assumed by paid health workers that they produce health; people out there are 'patients' (who suffer) and 'consumers' (who use health obtained from paid workers). Health workers have recently expressed a wish to give back to people responsibility and power in health care (Royal College of General Practitioners, 1982; DHSS, 1986; Ayton, 1987). But this is a misconception about how health is produced and who are the major producers (*see* Stacey, 1976). Mothers, working together with their children, maintain and promote their health.

In sum, we believe that it is important for paid workers to consider seriously the division of labour and responsibility between mothers, fathers, other carers and themselves. If they take into account seriously the work of parents, especially that of mothers, they may recognize that their own contribution is relatively minor, though on occasion important and even critical.

We have noted at several points that parents think (reasonably) that their knowledge should be acknowledged and their wishes listened to and responded to. Many studies support the finding that parents think services are not always satisfactory in these respects. For instance Dyson (1986) recently interviewed parents of mentally handicapped children; they said their knowledge was not made use of and their ideas about the services they needed were not sought by GPs and paediatricians. Dyson comments that services did not generally allow parents the opportunity to shape the services, which were handed down to them from on high. A salutary and provocative study!

Division of labour between paid workers

In at least two separate aspects the doctor's role differs from that of health visitors because, first it is technical, as opposed to social; and second, because it is responsive rather than interventionist. There is, therefore, a contrast between the role of the doctor and that of the health visitor. We had a very strong impression from health visitors that theirs was a conflict-ridden and stressful job. We suggest some explanations why this is so, and why the doctor's task is a simpler one.

The doctor's role is clearly delineated. They use their knowledge and skills to examine the child, diagnose, treat or refer. Not only did clinical medical officers believe they had higher status: this was reflected in the way they were treated. Doctors expect that, because of their higher status, life should be made easier for them and it is. Other workers, for example, clinic nurses and receptionists, smooth the way for them. Doctors tend on the whole to deal with physical aspects of health. Here there may be fairly good agreement about what is 'right' or 'wrong', although here also opinions may differ (*see* for example, Helman, 1984). Doctors have reserved for themselves the task of merely responding to the child being presented for examination. For mothers too, it is clearer what doctors can and cannot offer. In that situation, the contract between the doctor and the person seeking help is clearer. The position of the health visitor is more complex and, as a result, more stressful than that of the doctor. Health visitors deal with social and emotional health, where people's values are always relevant. Here there is less agreement than with physical aspects of health about what constitutes 'good' health and health care. So if health visitors believe that they know the 'right' way of rearing children, they are more likely than doctors to experience conflict with people. Unlike the doctor who provides a responsive service, the health visitor finds herself proferring an interventionist service. Her actions are 'pro-active', they are not usually initiated by the people she serves and she seeks out 'customers' for the services of doctors. Seeking out a population which may not want a service is no easy task. In contrast to the clear-cut role of the doctor, the health visitor has many roles. At any meeting between health visitors and mothers, mothers may differ from health visitors in their perception of the purpose of the encounter.

When we turn to the work of health visitors and social workers, we can see some dilemmas for both. As workers involved with the 'social', both health visitors and social workers are becoming less able to help with material resources, at a time when resources are scarcer. But health visitors have even less power than social workers. They do not have any *direct* access to money, housing and day care. They can only refer and must rely on the good-will and ability to help of other agencies. In that situation health visitors are perhaps even more likely than social workers to experience feelings of powerlessness and inability to be helpful.

ISSUES FOR DISCUSSION

1 Health visitors often say they use a social model of health. In practice do they and can they confront the social issues?
2 Parents may deal with GPs, clinical medical officers, health visitors, and social workers to help them with children's health care. Does the division of labour between the paid workers lead to services that are beneficial to parents and children?

FURTHER READING

Stacey M. (1976). *The health service consumer: a sociological misconception.* In The Sociology of the National Health Service. Social Review Monograph, University of Keele.

Stacey M. (1988). *The Sociology of Health and Healing.* London: Unwin Hyman. Chapters 13, 14 and 15.

Mayall B. (in press). The division of labour in early child care. *Journal of Social Policy.*

CHAPTER 7
SERVING A MULTI-ETHNIC COMMUNITY

In this chapter we explore aspects of service provision in relation to the idea of 'serving a community'. We discuss the extent to which health workers should take into account structural factors in providing health services. We look at this problem using two different approaches.

First we take the fact that Britain is a multi-ethnic society. Our data suggest that from the parents' point of view, material and structural factors in this society powerfully affect health care behaviour.

Secondly, we consider approaches to health education, and note two very different focuses: a focus on the individual and a focus on the community.

Finally, we discuss health service staff responses to the challenge of working in a plural and divided society.

BRITAIN AS A MULTI-ETHNIC SOCIETY

To start, we look at the implications for service-provision of Britain being a multi-ethnic society. Clearly this is a complex topic and here we have selected some important features.

Britain is a country with extremes of wealth and poverty. It is also a country which is plural in another important sense. Many people live in this country who have not been here for many generations. These are people with some other kind of identity or background, as well as, or instead of, identity as British. Health workers have the difficult task of somehow providing a service for this wide variety of people.

We present first the perspectives of mothers. They told us what it was like for them to be a mother in a multi-ethnic society. We shall then consider the response of health workers, and the kinds of construction which they put on the notion of serving a plural community. We shall finally set the opinions and the experience of mothers against the ways in which health workers approach their work in a multi-ethnic society.

LIVING IN MULTI-ETHNIC BRITAIN: MOTHERS' PERSPECTIVES

We chose our parent sample to reflect the multi-ethnic nature of one inner London Health Authority area. As can be seen in Table 1.1 (pp. 6–7), our sample comprised a variety of people from a large number of nationalities. Ethnic minorities in Britain are minorities in terms of their relatively small number and also in terms of power *vis-à-vis* the white indigenous population. It is important to note that minority groups are not homogeneous and not everyone who belongs to a minority is disadvantaged. However, in general, minorities, particularly Blacks, in Britain are disproportionately disadvantaged when compared to the white indigenous population. A recent (draft) document by the Health Visitors' Association (in press) reviews the literature on the topic and summarizes succinctly the position of ethnic minorities. Essentially, as a group, they are economically disadvantaged and they suffer from discrimination in important aspects of life: employment, housing, education and health. So they are more likely to experience both poverty and its effects on health (*see* also Brown, 1984).

We present here some general points made by the minority mothers in our sample on child-rearing, on their goals and on bringing up a child in Britain. Not surprisingly, all mothers shared the same aims; they wanted the best for their children. They were also trying to provide the best possible care for these children. Their ability to do so, however, was facilitated or hindered by certain factors.

Material problems

Many of these households faced difficulties: low paid jobs or unemployment, very poor housing conditions and financial difficulties. Money was the source of many worries and mothers gave us various accounts of how they attempted to economize. Women make sacrifices so as to provide for other members of the household, especially children (c.f. Graham, 1984).

I: 'Do you have any difficulties giving him good food?'
M: 'It depends on your husband's wages . . . if you work out like weekly when you go to the shop. If you don't buy sort of clothes or anything then you can afford to give him nice food.'

I: 'Have you found it difficult to manage with your husband out of work?'
M: 'Yes, it's very difficult but my sister-in-law she sometimes gives us some presents and if she is not giving us presents she is giving us money . . . But when it comes to pay the bills and these things then it's difficult, but I'm used to spend these things very safely. The gas, I try not to use them too much. I never watch TV, it costs too much. I listen to tape recorder only very rarely, but only my husband he used to watch TV, I never and I always think about these things. It's very difficult. Because we have to pay bills every 3 months. And for that we need money. It's difficult.'

Mothers also found 'healthy' food was expensive.

I: 'Do you find it easy to give her good food?'
M: 'It's difficult because sometimes when you go to the shops certain things you want it's very expensive. But in the house, I buy fruit every single day for her. Now if you look at my kitchen there's apples, there's bananas, but it's only for her, I don't touch it. I don't touch it at all. And with my meals they're like maybe meat and rice, maybe I'll have a salad now and then, but with her it would be a lot of vegetables like carrots, a bit of cabbage, turnip, parsnips and a few bits of potatoes and I'll put a few frozen peas in there and I'll give it to her because I have been bringing her up on a lot of vegetables and meat and she enjoys it.'

M: 'I find that things in the health shops are so expensive and those are the things that are right for you without any preservatives. Things with preservatives and stabilizers etc. They are the cheapest things in the shops, the tinned things, etc. and you know, which I think is so unfair, because you would think that the things without preservatives would be cheaper, don't you think so – the natural things are so expensive!'

Keeping children warm in the British climate was difficult for many households. People told us that their child slept with them in winter to keep warm; many economized by keeping only one room warm.

(Mother studying at home while child is at nursery talking about how she economizes on heating bills – this was an extremely cold winter.)
M: 'I am fortunate in that a lot of the times she is not there, like at the moment I have not got anything on (heating) but it's going to come on when I go to pick her up. When I am on my own I put a jumper on. When she comes home it's on until the time she goes to bed then it's

turned off again and then on again a little bit in the morning before we get up and just before we go.'

Poor housing conditions, inadequate playspace, unsafe housing and environment for their children were also causes for concern among many of the mothers we interviewed. Many believed that the damp and overcrowded conditions of their accommodation led to ill health and was hazardous to their children. Keeping children and their environment clean in old dirty housing was also difficult.

As discussed in Chapter 2, lack of day-care facilities hindered mothers who wished to earn money in order to improve child-care. Most mothers did not share the ideology that mothers of young children should not take up paid employment. They believed they had a role to contribute financially. Our sample of mothers contained people with high educational levels who either could not find paid work or were in low paid work, which did not reflect their qualifications and education.

Of course difficulties associated with low socio-economic status are not restricted to people from minority groups; they are shared with poor whites. But as one black writer graphically says, 'we may be in the same boat (as poor whites) but we (blacks) are on different decks', (Ottey, 1985). A provocative metaphor! Are minority groups, especially blacks, in the same boat as poor whites? To what extent can they be said to be on different decks?

Racism?

In our sample, very few mothers overtly expressed the view that they suffered from racism. Those who did were all British-born blacks, mostly highly educated. But while most mothers did not make a link between negative experience and racism this does not mean that they did not have to face racist practices. Their expectations of living in Britain might include experiencing racism as a 'normal' thing. One father casually remarked that his neighbourhood was 'OK because there are not many racial attacks'. His comment points to an experience of British life as racist and to expectations that life in Britain must be lived under the fear of attack.

It is striking that all minority mothers talked about Britain as an unfriendly society. This was a running theme in their accounts; unfriendliness affected their quality of life. This problem was especially acute for those mothers who had been here for less than 10 years and mostly had few or no relatives in this country.

> (This mother is talking about life in Britain.)
> *I*: 'Do you know people?'
> *M*: 'Oh no, . . . I think English people, they don't talk. They don't like to talk to others unless it's for work. If they have some work then they'll talk. Otherwise they never. They never say hello, nothing.'
> *I*: 'We are less friendly people?'
> *M*: 'Yes, very less friendly. Because I have been to Mexico and they are a very friendly people and even Americans are very friendly and even if they don't know you they say hello to you, but English don't.'

> (Another mother born in England is talking about her neighbourhood.)
> *M*: 'People in the streets as I say it's all down to making an effort to smile or something. In England . . . I know I'm Cypriot, which makes a difference. I've seen what it's like in Cyprus and over here. Like in Cyprus like you get out of your door in the morning, hello, how are you, come in for coffee, how are the children . . . in England there's nothing like that. Everybody minds their own business. You might pass someone in the street and they won't even look at you straight out in the eyes. And also I don't feel safe in the streets. You hear so many things, like mugging people, they pick up their children, they throw them on the floor, they kick them, they do things like that – this really scares me a lot because I keep feeling this is going to happen to me, so when I do go out I don't just go by myself to the shop, I go with my husband.'

Health visitors said they often recommended 'mother and toddler' groups to women as a means of making friends. Minority mothers found however, they were not necessarily accepted by white mothers.

> (This highly educated black mother is recounting her experience at a local mother and toddler group.)
> *I*: 'Do you like it yourself?'
> *M*: 'For me there's no enjoyment.'
> *I*: 'You don't meet anybody?'
> *M*: 'No, I don't, there are just certain groups and they see each other, I think they know each other.'

She went on to say how in such a setting no one talked to her and she was not accepted by the others.

Mothers had also found services were ethnocentric.

> *M*: 'You find that most of these books or whatever they are so English

geared – you don't necessarily . . . I mean I would not sort of go out and buy an English menu for her and a different thing for myself – I can't afford it you know, and I think it's silly, because she is not going to be eating like that all her life, so she may as well eat like that from now. I mean a lot of the food really, I mean the guide, they are very English – they are sort of biased in a way. It's not like they write either you have potato or yam. It's just potato you know.'

One mother we interviewed talked about her experience as a black nurse in Britain.

'On the wards where I worked you would find that probably . . . I mean 80% black people or a certain percentage of Indian, Chinese or whatever and then you find maybe that there is one or two English people, but the food is basically English through and through. I mean it's not as though it goes through phases it goes like that all the time. So it's sort of the health service I guess, maybe they just don't think about it.'

The mothers who talked overtly about racism related negative experiences they had encountered. This mother – a student in higher education – felt patronized by health workers, who linked skin colour and ethnic minority status with low intelligence.

'I think a few of them, presume that you are a bit thick or a bit stupid. I can't describe it . . . like you know . . . you are very naive and I think there a lot of people now who are not that naive at all . . . I think sometimes the way they talk to you as though you were very stupid, which I think . . . it's not the talking, it's how they do it . . .'

Minority mothers experienced poverty and had poor housing; they could not find day-care places for children; and they experienced living in an unfriendly and at times hostile society. In addition there were other circumstances which shaped their lives in Britain.

Social networks

Most mothers in our sample stressed the importance of continual contact with other people, especially their own mothers and sisters. They particularly needed their own mothers when they had a child. But for many, especially those who had arrived in Britain in recent years, these significant people were not in the country.

'Yes, I have always believed that especially with a first child, a mother needs her own mother with her, not with her but that she may ask advice; I would have been so happy if my mother was nearer to me, she would have helped me with Ahmed and it would have been much easier.'

'We miss our parents and our senior sisters and brothers, relatives that are well experienced because it costs quite a lot to phone (Nigeria). Once in a while, we phone, and they phone us sometimes, but because of the cost . . . but it's better, because when you write, it is long before a reply comes back.'

In an often tight budget, mothers allowed for overseas telephone calls, in order to feel nearer to significant relatives. But as some said telephone calls were also problematic. They could not confide in their own parents about problems and ill health. Parents were too far away to help or would be made too anxious. So sharing their anxieties with people who mattered was not possible for many mothers. By contrast few white majority mothers had relatives at a distance and even if so, contacts and visits were obviously easier.

The experience of migration

Those who had been in Britain for less than 10 years were especially disadvantaged with respect to social networks. The experience of migration had many profound effects on their lives. Lifestyles changed drastically. For example we had a highly qualified black woman who had worked in scientific research in her own country, came here to accompany her husband, but was unable to find employment. Lack of day-care facilities hindered her search for work. She was extremely isolated and lonely. Many mothers suffered from intense loneliness. One woman illustrated this by saying how she and her child waited all day 'for my husband to come in. When we hear the key in the door – oh what a relief'.

Except for those who were in paid work, contact with the white indigenous population consisted almost solely of meetings with health service staff, health visitors, clinical medical officers and GPs. For example, a Chinese woman appeared completely isolated from British society. Her life revolved round her child, servicing an extended household which ran a 'take away' restaurant. Members of that household, including her husband, worked from 9 a.m. to 2–3 a.m. every day. Her contacts with the outside world were mainly outings to the Chinese area of London, to shop for food or to see the Chinese doctor. It is particularly striking that when her child was born this woman had been very appreciative of the health visitor's visits.

Lack of information and 'know-how'

Several women lacked basic knowledge and know-how about British society. One believed that health visitors were concerned only with babies, not with toddlers. Indeed she had not seen her own health visitor since her child was about 3 months old. She also did not know that she could initiate contact with preventive health workers; she attended clinic only when sent an appointment.

During our interviews we found ourselves filling in gaps in people's knowledge. We told confused parents about different types of nurseries and child-care groups, for example playgroups, mother and toddler groups, day nurseries and nursery schools and how to find them. We also told people how to find a dentist, about local community groups, job finding agencies, parks, citizens' advice bureaux, bus routes. No doubt women gradually learn from talking with staff at health clinics and so on – and these mothers were all 'good clinic attenders'. But it was no-one's job specifically to help them find their way in Britain.

Importance of health workers

Women new to this country relied more than others on health workers because they lacked contact with their own relatives. An interesting finding was that they were strikingly more positive about health visitors than others (Table 7.1). They also viewed the services differently. They were the women who stressed benevolence while most of the others viewed health workers as policing and controlling (Table 7.2).

Another interesting point is that relative newcomers emphasized the personality of the health visitor even more than other mothers did. Friendliness was especially important. A study in Bradford found that Pathan women assessed health visitors in terms of their personal rather than their occupational qualities (Currer, 1983). In an unfriendly society friendly health workers were especially welcome.

To sum up, minority mothers suffered even more than other

Table 7.1 Mother's evaluation of health visitors by number of years in UK

	Minority sample Years in Britain			White majority sample	n
	0–5	6–10	11+		
Positive comments about HV including personality	7	4	5	2	18
Both positive and negative	2		1	4	7
Negative comments only			5	2	7
No comment (does not know HV well enough)	0	1	0	0	1
n	9	5	11	8	33

Table 7.2 Mother's perception of major role of health visitors by number of years in UK

	Minority sample Years in Britain			White majority sample	n
	0–5	6–10	11+		
Sees HV's *major* role to be:					
Policing households and checking mother's standards	3	3	8	8	22
Someone who gives advice	6	2	3	0	11
n	9	5	11	8	33

mothers from problems such as lack of day-care facilities, low income and poor quality housing. They felt Britain was unfriendly, hostile, or racist. They missed their own relatives and some lacked know-how to negotiate a satisfactory place for themselves and their children in British society. Recent migration compounded these problems. Newcomers relied more heavily on health workers to compensate for lack of informal network.

PERSPECTIVES OF HEALTH WORKERS ON WORKING IN A MULTI-ETHNIC SOCIETY

Evidence such as we quote suggests that it will be demanding for health and welfare workers of many kinds to provide a service in a multi-ethnic society. How did the health workers view the society, the people they served, and their work? Many health visitors and clinical medical officers emphasized the importance of culture. Although all of them (except two health visitors) endorsed the view that ethnic minorities had the right to maintain their own culture they had difficulties in implementing this view in their practice. They felt at a loss, especially with 'Asian' culture. They believed that it was a gap in their own knowledge about minority culture which created work difficulties. If they knew enough about ethnic minority culture, they felt that they would be in a position to advise appropriately.

There are several distinctive features of this conceptualization. First, culture is seen as a discrete entity that is readily identified and (often) is unchanging. It is independent of people's socioeconomic circumstances. Secondly, many health workers explained the behaviour of 'an ethnic minority' person solely in terms of this culture. Generally both health visitors and clinical medical officers perceived the culture of ethnic minorities as problematic. All except two health visitors discussed ethnic minorities as constituting a problem to them as workers. It was more difficult to work with these people as they did not conform to their norms and their expectations. For some health visitors it was an easy step to go from this perception of culture as a problem to negative stereotyping of certain groups. For example, they associated harsh discipline with 'West Indians' and 'West Africans', and 'Asian' women were dominated by their men and both unwilling and unable to socialize with the majority population. Our data are supported by Donovan (1986) and Pearson (1986) who document how workers in positions of power such as doctors act according to negative stereotyping of certain groups.

In the following example, note how the health visitor slips from these generalizing explanations into blaming the individual.

(A health visitor discussing the local Asian mothers.)
HV: 'We have difficulties getting the men to let their wives learn English and they tend to be perhaps stuck at home all day with their own set of friends or family. And they don't get out much, they don't seem to want them to learn any more about this type of life over here. And they do get lonely but . . . there are facilities here if they were only interested.'

The following example highlights the emphasis health workers placed on cultural differences.

I: 'Do you think your colour affects how you deliver the services?'
HV: 'Yes, I think it most probably does. Before I came here I visited – I was actually visiting Indian families not very many of them and I think I actually – I think I deal with a much more negative attitude, because I

didn't expect them to take any notice of me and also I was very reluctant to tread on any toes, you know, I suppose I was reluctant to go against – it was while I was training and doing my supervised practice so I was you know, very hesitant anyway, but that I was extra hesitant – you know, going to the Indian families, because I was very conscious that I didn't know enough about their culture. It worked out very well, because there were two – the two brothers had had these two girls and they had all lived in the same house with grandma and it seemed to me silly to keep going in feeling like this, so I had a talk with them about it and said you know, that I would like to offer what I've got to offer and what we offer to all families, but I didn't want to offend their religion or their customs and so if I said anything wrong would they please forgive me and tell me about it, which worked very well. We had instances like somebody had told them to put their children on SMA and SMA contains beef fat and they were – really couldn't do it and then I was in a quandary because I knew that and they didn't and I didn't know whether to share it with them and suggest they changed the milk or whether to . . . you know.'

I: 'What did you do in that particular instance?'

HV: 'I agreed with them. I said to them that – I went in one day and they had put the babies on SMA and I went back and I looked it up and I realized it had beef fat in, then some people said to me just let it slide and I thought well I would have hated it if I thought that it had been something that you know it was against my religion and somebody had known that I was doing it wrong so I went along and I said to them that well, you know, I had gone away and looked up and found that this had it in and you know that it was then up to them and in fact all that happened was they changed the milk, but that did actually change my relationship with them, because they knew that I was really, you know, trying not to offend them, I think.'

In line with the emphasis on 'culture', as a problem health workers believed that a solution was for them to receive better training and education about people's 'cultures'. If they acquired more knowledge about the cultural traits of minority groups this would enable them to give a good service. This perspective ignores the dynamic character of culture. People's culture changes through time and space and, as we have said, our small sample contained twenty different nationalities. These are also divided along class, educational and regional lines. Is it therefore feasible, even if this were desirable, for health workers to learn about the culture of minorities? Focus on 'culture' may also be a substitute for recognizing the serious problems people face in living an adequate life here. As the mothers illustrated, structural problems in an unfriendly, hostile, racist society were the important issues.

Health workers emphasized the distinctive cultural practices of minority groups as though these were the most important features of good care. Mothers did give us examples – not many – of different child-care practices. For example, this mother valued exercising her child's limbs and also stressed skin care:

> 'I always rub her down mornings and evenings. That's . . . cream her skin with cow butter or baby oil or sometimes both or olive oil. That's done everyday regardless of weekend or whatever she gets that and I find it makes her legs supple as well.'

Some British child-care practices may look odd judged by international standards, for example, the concern with toilet training. Another example is the practice of putting young children to bed very early in the evenings. As anyone who has travelled to Southern Europe will have noted, this is not the practice in many other countries. Isolating mothers in the sole company of their children is also not a common practice. A study of six cultures found that only in New England, USA was this the practice (Mintern and Lambert, 1984).

Many health visitors and all clinical medical officers said that they were unable to communicate with some minority groups because of language difficulties. Interpreters were more widely available in the county area than in London. However, a few health visitors had reservations about the quality of interpreters. An ethnic minority health visitor believed that health workers used language as an easy excuse for not attempting to communicate with some people. It is important also to remember that language barrier is a feature only

Table 7.3 Health visitors' (HVs) and clinical medical officers' perspectives on working in a multi-ethnic society

	London HVs	County HVs	Clinical medical officers
Culture discussed as a major issue	20	16	6
Racism discussed as a major issue	8	0	0
Racism mentioned as a possible issue	5	4	0
Structural issues of poverty, housing etc. discussed	2 implicitly	0	0
n	28	20	11

with a few minority people. For many people from ethnic minorities and for most Blacks there is no such language barrier. There are, therefore, other important reasons for difficulties which arise in encounters between health and welfare workers and ethnic minority people.

As can be seen from Table 7.3 while most health workers stressed culture few health visitors and no clinical medical officer identified racism as an issue. Some health visitors suggested that this was a topic which did not warrant attention.

> *HV*: 'And racial issues are discussed. I feel very strongly that that is very often, and so does my colleague, taken wrongly, because very often I loved to visit my Pakistani families – I really enjoyed it, because there are lots of families that are really, really lovely. And there isn't an issue at all of the racial thing, at all. I think it's made up – I really do feel it's, it's made into something which is really basically not there, because if you're a caring person, if you do become a nurse or a health visitor or a doctor, if you didn't care for any colour, creed or whatever, class, so I think we're really making a mountain out of something which is not there. Really, I absolutely think we're going the wrong way about – and making a problem because people are now, because we're talking about it (they) think they are discriminated about. And they're not.'

Others said that society could be racist, but health visitors were not, although they were at times uncertain how people from ethnic minorities experienced everyday situations. This next health visitor is talking about working in a multi-ethnic society.

> *I*: 'Do you think your colour affects how people treat you – as a health visitor?'
>
> *HV*: 'As a health visitor. I don't think it does no, really, as a health visitor going in I mean I don't think it does. I think the coloured population
> feel as a whole in the UK that it affects them and I'm sure it does, I'm sure we still have a lot of prejudices and I think jobs and many things that are treated differently but I don't honestly think that health visitors going in or – into a home or in a clinic – I think they, yes, I think possibly in the clinic when they are very much in the minority – one sitting in a clinic situation and I think that's why you do get clinics where there are many more because they feel more comfortable, but since most health visitors are not of ethnic minorities I think we must feel that for them it doesn't make any difference. But I think it would be nice for them to see more of their own race if you like so that if they wish to relate more comfortably then they could.'

The health visitors who identified racism as an important issue believed that it shaped the quality of life of minority groups. They also felt that it was at times difficult for them as white majority people to be sensitive to others. They often commented that they tried their best to be sensitive to racism, but said that it was difficult for them to know whether they were successful or not. They suggested that health visitors should receive training in racial awareness.

> *HV*: 'I'm sure I find myself shouting at people who don't speak English and doing the typical things that you do to people who don't understand English and I'm sure, sometimes you think, "Oh God, why do they do that . . .", which you might not think of from somebody from your own culture. I mean I can honestly say that I try not to let it affect the way I deliver my services . . . but I think if somebody assessed me, they would probably pick out glaring faults that I'm totally unaware of really.'

A few health visitors acknowledged that it could be difficult to get ethnic minorities accepted by indigenous mothers.

> (Ethnic minority health visitor talking about health visiting in multi-ethnic Britain.)
> *I*: 'Anything you can do as health visitors?'
> *HV*: 'If I say by, you know, trying to get the mothers (white British mothers) to be a little bit more involved with them. In a subtle way. Um – unless I think the mothers are, unless these families are directly involved with the ethnic minority they'll never actually find out, so it's to actually try and get one family to befriend one, the one who's in need of help. Rather than um – I was just thinking if I, rather than trying to get a similar race to befriend them. Yes, I think one could promote that. But you know, it needs working on. It's willingness on the part of the English family to befriend and to learn about other people.'

To summarize, while mothers emphasized the material difficulties they faced, the health workers, except two London HVs, did not link the experience of minority groups to their economic position. Most health workers also did not express any recognition that mothers found British society unfriendly, hostile or racist. Unlike mothers, they focused on differences in cultural practices, which they often perceived in a negative way. Thus their main focus was on the individual and not on societal structures.

EXPLANATORY MODELS FOR HEALTH AND TARGETS FOR HEALTH EDUCATION

Like anybody else, health workers provide explanations to account for 'good' health and 'ill' health. These beliefs may have profound implications for the service they offer. We have noted how health workers had a tendency to give less weight to material factors and to focus on the individual. In the second section of this chapter we consider these explanatory models and how these can lead to different approaches in health education.

Ill health has been attributed to a number of causes. Here we are concerned with two opposing models. The first one suggests that, now that medicine has conquered many life-threatening diseases, individual behaviour is the biggest factor responsible for health status. This has been the notion underlying official preventive documents in the last few years. The document *Prevention and Health – Everybody's Business* (DHSS, 1976) exemplifies this way of thinking. Although mention is made of material factors the focus is on changing the behaviour of the irresponsible or misinformed (or both) individual. This model rests on certain premises: the individual's health would improve if he changed his lifestyle, and the individual has power and sufficient control over his life to change his behaviour. Women writers have pointed out that the pronoun 'he' is problematic. Women and not men are singled out to change the behaviour and the lifestyle of people; they are assigned responsibility not only to change their own habits, but as wives and mothers to change the behaviour of men and children. For example campaigns for the prevention of coronary heart disease in men have been aimed at women (Graham, 1984).

In the field of child health, women commentators (e.g. Graham, 1979,b) draw our attention to the fact that although it is assumed women must carry responsibility, they are rarely given the resources to help them do the work (Land, 1983). The critics of the behavioural and individualistic school point out that the important factors affecting children's lives cannot be tackled through individual behaviour. In child health care, the absence of day-care facilities for mothers and the lack of financial support to mothers illustrate how social policy, while relying on the rhetoric that mothers should be more responsible people, does not however practically help them in that task. Women often do not have control over the resources of the household. Studies point to the unequal distribution of resources within households: wives and mothers have to manage on what men choose to give them (Wilson, 1987) and women lack power to change behaviour (Charles and Kerr, 1986). Women are further disadvantaged if they are not themselves in paid employment. Sacrifices feature highly in the lives of many women, and sacrifice usually means self-sacrifice to enable children to have their due.

The second model emphasizes the effect of societal factors on health. Here primacy is given to environmental and 'structural' features such as housing, money, sanitation in promoting or damaging health. The Black Report (Townsend and Davidson, 1982) has been the most important document in recent years to argue for the link between socioeconomic status and health. At its extreme this model suggests that large scale redistribution of resources such as money and housing known to enhance life chances are the best ways of promoting health. Parents generally lack control over important factors affecting their health and that of their children – poverty, pollution in the environment, their housing, their work situations, the inability to obtain suitable work and the lack of sufficient day-care facilities for children. For women bringing up children, their 'structural' inequalities in society need to be tackled and efforts made to provide the type of resources which would facilitate child-care. Such resources would include job maintenance, income maintenance, child allowances, adequate playspace and suitable environment in their own homes, and practical help from public agencies, especially day-care provision for young children.

Explanatory models held by health workers

Perhaps, not surprisingly, given the traditional emphasis by doctors and nurses on an individualistic approach to health promotion, health workers in our study showed a strong tendency to give individualistic explanations. Health workers are trained in a framework that emphasizes consideration of people as individuals, apart from their social and economic context. This training encourages health workers to emphasize individualistic solutions to health problems: doctors give you pills, health visitors give you advice. While all the health workers in both samples acknowledged that social factors affected health and could either help or hinder child health care, many downplayed these and blamed individuals for not taking active steps to promote their better health (*see* for example quote in Chapter 3, pp. 49–50).

We suggest here some points for discussion and give a few examples of the views of health workers. The examples we give may help to clarify to the readers how we divided health workers into the groups in Table 7.4.

Table 7.4 Explanatory models of health workers

	London HVs	County HVs	CMOs
Individualistic model	13	11	4
Mixed model – both individualistic and structuralist explanations	7	8	6
Structuralist model	8	1	1
n	28	20	11

HVs: health visitors; CMOs: clinical medical officers

Table 7.4 shows differences between the three sets of workers. London health visitors were faced daily by dramatic evidence of the constraints imposed on people by material conditions. The only county health visitor who did favour a structuralist model had previously worked in a deprived inner city area. So it seems very likely that working experience plays a part in perceptions of relevant explanatory factors. Many clinical medical officers acknowledged the importance of material factors, but thought these were outside their realm – health visitors dealt with these aspects of health and health care.

Those health workers, the majority, who adopted an *individualistic* approach tended to mention structural issues, but then quickly went on to blame the individual.

Here this health visitor provides explanations for accidents rooted in the mother's ignorance and motivation.

> *I*: 'I expect you know that children in social class V are more likely than other children to have serious accidents. Why do you think that is?'
> *HV*: 'Just because they're neglectful and they don't take the right precautions. I think underneath they know but they just can't be bothered. It's part and parcel of this business, the baby has got to go down having been fed, it's got to go down and sleep until the next feed and that carries on while the child is older and the child is sort of

crawling about and pulling things down and they don't really keep as much as an eye on it.'

Next is an example of a *'mixed'* view: a health visitor presenting both individualistic and structuralistic explanations, giving equal weight to both.

HV: 'Quite often the less well off mothers will spend a lot of money at the chemist buying jars and packets whereas really with not an awful lot of money they can probably make a meal for themselves and any other children or whoever and modify that to suit the baby and it won't cost as much and probably nutritionally wise it's just as sound if not better. And I think one hopes to make their awareness of using their limited income to the best – you know – to be quite effective, but one does feel terribly ineffective when you go to a house and they haven't had the Giro cheque that was due 5 or 6 days ago and this sort of thing. And they literally had no money, that is their entire income and they are so dependent on it and if it doesn't arrive and it really is – that is a problem.'

'Structuralist' health visitors gave primacy to social and environmental factors as influencing health and explained behaviour in those terms.

This again, is about the cause of accidents:

HV: 'I think I'd come back to housing. They live in poorer housing, high rise flats and you know they don't have the money to or they have difficulty getting sort of fireguards and those sort of safety equipments. Overcrowding that's another situation. Possibly mum leaves the child alone, you know she has no choice, she has to go and do something . . . I think mostly it's the environment, it's not anything to do with their intelligence or their caring. It's just that in their situation they are in, and also the fact that if you live in council housing the repairs get done later, locks on the windows take ages, a broken window will take 6 months to get repaired.'

Another structuralist talking about clinic attendance:

HV: 'Parents from social classes I and II can't wait to get into clinic as soon as they've had their child. Parents from other social classes, yes, they are keen and they value it, but they have not got transport, it's a long way to come, very inadequate bus service and if you've got five other children what do you do with the other four while you bring one to clinic . . . it's just a different perspective. They want the best for their children, I certainly would never deny that, but actually the uptake differs because of all these other factors that are involved. With social class I you've got two cars, you've got, you know you can arrange to drop your child at somebody's on the way, it's two minutes in the car, it's no problem. When you have not got transport it's a very different kettle of fish.'

DISCUSSION

It is difficult for any of us fully to understand how others experience living in Britain. Most paid health care workers are both middle class and white and their work involves helping women who may be working class and black. We have tried to show how women's experiences in general and child-care practices in particular are shaped by large-scale factors – such as poor housing and day-care policies, and including their experience of British society as hostile and/or racist.

For the paid worker it seems there are two linked problems in their work in a multi-ethnic society: to recognize the strength of the influence of social factors in shaping people's lives; and to provide a service that acts on this recognition.

As we have suggested in earlier chapters, British social policies and practices seem to us to be hostile to the well-being of mothers and children in general, but working class and black people face a greater number of, and more acute problems. The construction which radical writers have placed on the experience of minorities helps us understand what seems to be lacking in the understanding of health workers about Britain as a multi-ethnic society.

For example, on the issue of racism, writers point out that colonial history is important in explaining the racism black people experience. Throughout the centuries they have been depicted as inferior, and this is reflected in British society today. (For a discussion *see* Husband, 1982.) Writers on racism also point out how government action – by both major political parties, culminating in the Nationality Act 1981 – has made racism not only legitimate but also respectable in Britain.

Racism determines to a large extent the experience and position of minorities in British society. For instance, in the NHS although black people are extensively employed, very few blacks are in positions of power and authority (Akinsanya, 1988). Detailed studies have shown how discrimination against minority groups occurs during pregnancy, and that beliefs and practices in maternity services are racist. Another example is that it is black people – often British born – rather than whites – including white foreigners – who have to prove to hospital staff that they have a right to be treated under the NHS (*see* Phoenix, 1989).

Minority groups are therefore disadvantaged through an ethnocentric and at times racist health service and in a social context where racism and discrimination are prevalent. For instance in preventive child health care (*see*, for example, Brent CHC, 1981) while screening for phenylketonuria is routinely offered to all babies, screening for sickle cell anaemia, a disease of minorities, is not so offered. Here a public health solution was adopted for a general health problem, but not for a 'minority' problem. Asian communities have repeatedly asked for fortification of their flour with vitamins A and D, a request which has been turned down by officials. Yet rickets was eliminated in the post-war period in the white indigenous population by adding these vitamins to foodstuffs such as margarine. Here public health solutions were adopted only in respect of foods consumed mainly by the majority population. Asian mothers are blamed for failing to give their children vitamin supplements. We live in a society where racism shapes the lives of many people. A few of our mothers talked in terms of racism, but most expressed their unhappiness by saying they lived in an unfriendly, hostile society. For many of them racism is a 'normal' part of their experience, and it affects the quality of their lives and their health.

Material factors are also important in affecting people's lives and particularly their health. Therefore it is important for health workers to confront this issue. There is a danger for health workers such as health visitors who work *with* individuals to perceive problems as arising mainly or solely *from* individual failings. Since the publication of the Black Report (*see* Townsend and Davidson, 1982), health workers cannot ignore the argument that there are strong links between socioeconomic status and health. To see problems only in individualistic terms may throw blame on people for events and behaviours for which they cannot be held totally responsible. Health education aimed solely at changing individual behaviour may be both inappropriate and ineffective (*see* Naidoo, 1986).

In an important paper, Crawford (1977) discusses the assignment of blame for ill health and the complete responsibility for good health on the individual. He argues that this results in an ideology of 'victim blaming', in a social context where much concern about health can be attributed to structural and environmental factors. He warns that this 'victim blaming ideology' serves to instruct 'people to be individually responsible at a time when they are becoming less capable as individuals of controlling their health environment'.

This approach does not reject the value of individual health education and promotion but suggests that this alone is not sufficient. In any analysis of health, social factors and constraints need to be taken into consideration. Working on a one-to-one basis may hide the fact that many issues and problems are socially constructed.

To take on structural issues, however, is no easy task. The clinical medical officers were shielded by their working conditions. They by-passed the task, by arguing that social issues were not their province. Health visitors felt powerless when faced with poor housing, poverty, unemployment and the subordinate position of women. The way most health visitors in our study dealt with these structural problems was twofold. *Firstly*, although they acknowledged the societal factors affecting health, they focused on the failings of the individual, or what they perceived to be such failings. They attempted to change the behaviour of the individual and paid little attention to the fact that many of the women they met lacked power to control their lives because of societal constraints. *Secondly*, they attempted to get women to accept their fate. They offered counsel and support to women so that their lives would become – they hoped! – slightly more bearable. Their role was to help mothers adjust to their circumstances. But many of the mothers we interviewed did not wish to adjust to the policy *makers'* belief of their place and their role. They wanted to change their way of life, but found it difficult to do so.

To provide a service to people is a challenge to workers in a society stratified by class, gender and ethnicity. Health workers may wish to explore ways of developing a 'sociological imagination' where the link is made between private problems and public issues (Wright Mills, 1970). This enables health workers to understand that what appears to be an individual problem may often be a societal problem. In that situation to be solely concerned with the individual level does not resolve that problem. Therefore health workers need to find ways of guarding against individualizing problems and of dealing with these public issues. This may involve developing new approaches in their work.

ISSUES FOR DISCUSSION

1   Should health and welfare workers tackle racism? How?

2 Do health and welfare workers have a role to play in working for social change?

FURTHER READING

Graham, H. (1979b). Prevention and health: every mother's business. A comment on child health policies in the 1970s. In *The Sociology of the Family*. Social Monograph 25, University of Keele.

Husband, C. (ed.) *'Race' in Britain – Continuity and Change*. (1982). London: Hutchinson and Co.

Rodmell, S. and Watt, A. (eds.) (1986). *The Politics of Health Education – Raising the Issues*. London: Routledge and Kegan Paul.

Farrant W., Russell J. (1986). *The Politics of Health Information*. 'Beating heart disease' as a case study of Health Education Council Publications. London: University of London Institute of Education.

Harrison P. (1983). *Inside the Inner City – Life Under the Cutting Edge*. Harmondsworth: Penguin Books. A powerful account of what it is like living in an inner city area.

Naidoo J. (1986). *Limits to Individualism*. In Rodmell and Watt – *see* above.

Pearson M. (1986). *Racist Notions of Ethnicity and Culture in Health Education*. In Rodmell and Watt – *see* above.

CHAPTER 8
DISCUSSION

SOME THOUGHTS ON THE STUDY DATA

In this book we have tried to give a voice to parental and health staff perspectives on the work of promoting and maintaining child health, and on the functions and usefulness of preventive health services. We think it is important for health and welfare workers to consider their own work in the context of these perspectives. Our assumption is that services staff should make a point of working towards understanding their own and other people's perspectives so that they may offer a responsive service, within the limits of their remit.

Parents' accounts make it very clear that giving good care is highly dependent on the social, physical and economic context within which they live. For instance, some parents lacked the money to give their child good food, and the housing and neighbourhood to provide a clean and warm environment and the opportunity to exercise in the fresh air. Some mothers knew their child was unhappy because she had no friends. Some missed their own mothers and sisters from whom best to learn the skills and knowledge they needed for good child-care. Some mothers, and fathers, who had long hours of paid work away from home, wanted more time to interact with their children.

However, for those parents who faced many difficulties in living a good life themselves and in giving their child good care, the saving grace was the child herself. Loving the child and interacting with her was the rewarding part of life. As the child grew older, the physical work of child-care was becoming less onerous and demanding, and the child's contribution to relationships with her parents and with others was developing. So parents of the toddlers were enjoying being with their children and helping the children learn and develop as individuals and as social beings.

It was very clear to us that people's lives and those of their children are powerfully affected by social policies and practices. As we have

140

noted, social policies and practices endorse and promote certain models of fatherhood, motherhood and childhood and, in particular, policies on mothers' paid work and on day-care are for many mothers a serious hindrance to the achievement of a good life. British policies and practices on ethnic minorities and new immigrants are also damaging to people's attempts to live well in Britain.

What is striking in this study, as it was in the earlier one, is that the power of these policies and practices to control people's lives and to affect their well-being varies very much, and varies systematically according to the position of the parents in the social, economic and ethnic structures of the country. To put it briefly and schematically, white indigenous middle-class parents have most of the advantages and black, immigrant working-class parents least.

We expand here a bit on that simplified picture. White indigenous middle-class parents can afford to buy their way to an acceptable way of life. Thus, they buy day-care for their children, and mothers as well as fathers do well paid jobs. They may even be able to choose jobs which allow for some flexibility and time to care for their children as they think fit. They can also afford housing to suit their household. Being able to afford phones and cars, and having some freedom of movement, probably helps these parents establish and maintain good social networks.

White working class mothers have less control over some important aspects of their lives and those of their children. Poverty is a serious and growing problem in Britain: it particularly affects old people and households with young children (*see* e.g. Walker and Walker, 1987). But poorly educated working class parents cannot earn enough both to improve the household's resources and to buy good day-care. In addition, as some evidence suggests, working class women may be early exposed to and internalize the view that, as mothers, all their time should be spent at home with their children. Poor people, at any rate in big cities, are likely to have to accept at best housing in flats, without gardens, and this they see as a major constraint on good child-rearing.

Our study suggests that when we consider factors affecting family life and functioning among ethnic minorities and new immigrants, some factors cut across simple social class divisions. Parents' perception that English people are unfriendly and social contacts difficult, cuts across both class divisions and divisions according to length of residence in Britain. It was, however, more highly educated women, who also had longer residence here, who construed their experiences as experiences of racism. We also found that if one takes middle class women (whether white, black, indigenous or immigrant), then it was the newer immigrants who were unable to solve the linked problems of finding paid work and day-care. It seemed that poor knowledge of the system, which includes having poor social networks in the neighbourhood, provides one explanation for this. The unwillingness of agencies to take these women's enquiries seriously also seemed to be a factor.

However, while hostile or racist policies and practices affected the well-being of most ethnic minority mothers, and their opportunities for advancement, it was also the case that those with the least education, and those whose own and husband's work experience was in manual jobs, were most severely constrained of all as regards their standards of living. They lived in poor housing, husbands worked very long, often 'unsocial hours'; if the women did paid work it was physically exhausting work, also with long hours. Day-care at minders, relatives and friends was very much second-best to what they wanted – nursery care, where the child would be cared for in surroundings that compensated for poor housing at home and by trained, reliable staff. Some of these women were very conscious of the fact that their wish to educate themselves and thus better their chances in Britain, was frustrated by poor provision for themselves and their children, and by their own poverty.

Our sample was deliberately chosen to reflect some of the demographic characteristics of our multi-ethnic society and it encapsulates some of that society's extremes, in terms of people's material prosperity and their satisfaction with their way of life. The data from our study provide some details on some important mechanisms whereby there is variation in people's access to the means of achieving good health. The data perhaps help to explain some of that from large scale social class analyses, as reported for instance in the Black Report (Townsend and Davidson, 1982) and in studies providing analyses by ethnicity such as that by the Runnymede Trust and Radical Statistics Group (1980).

In sum then, major problems the parents faced stemmed from large-scale social, economic and racist policies and practices.

As regards health services, our data indicated that mothers welcomed the existence of both curative and preventive services and had no hesitation in using them when they felt the need. They went for diagnosis, cure, information and advice. They appreciated a parent-led responsive service, where staff listened to them, gave them time and were caring in their behaviour. They found it useful to discuss in detail issues such as immunization and the child's development. Some viewed services as secretive and even threatening, since health workers wrote and kept records on the child. Major criticisms were, as in many studies, that opening hours were inadequate, and waiting times long; parents did not always feel the attention given was thorough. The evidence suggests too that parents need information about the services, and parents new to the area need a great deal of information to help them find their way in our complex society. They accepted that health services had a part to play in overseeing child-care practices, but they rejected the idea that staff had a right to impose their own views and initiate health education with them.

What kind of service do health workers give to parents of under-5s? Some doctors argue that parental social and economic problems are right outside their remit. Most of 'our' clinical medical officers specifically and deliberately limited their work to the physical and developmental assessment of children and to answering mothers' questions. They saw this as a good use of the doctors' skills and time, and as what, essentially, they were paid to do. Since they worked in a team setting with health visitors, they were able to suggest that health visitors should deal with social problems. A few health visitors also operated on this model. As one strikingly said, she explained to mothers, 'You wouldn't ask the housing department for help on breast-feeding, so don't come to me for help on housing'. (She did say however that she referred people to the housing department.) This model assumes, essentially, that health status can be assessed and help can be given by health workers independently of consideration of people's social and economic circumstances. It is responsive within the limits of the workers' perception of their skills and their remit. It does not claim to offer more than it can deliver and therefore has the important merit of being a clear-cut service.

A model of health service work that stands at an extreme from this one is that discussed and promoted in recent papers on health visiting (Ayton, 1987) and adopted by some community health workers. There are certain key assumptions behind this model. *Firstly*, it is assumed that people's health status needs to be considered in the context of their social and economic circumstances. *Secondly*, for improvement in health to take place, it is seen as necessary for people to be active in the process of identifying health and social problems and needs, and in working towards improvement. Thus in practice, such workers will seek to identify, together with groups of local people, their health problems, and the opportunities and constraints in the neighbourhood which affect their chances of achieving good health. Here the paid worker is responding to the expressed concerns of the people and working with them to solve problems. In the course of this health care work, both paid and unpaid health workers are likely to be brought face to face with intractable social and political issues. Drennan's (1986) account of her work in a north London district gives a full and very readable account of this kind of approach, of her progress, successes and difficulties.

These two models are very different in their assumptions and practices, and while the first is accepted and supported by health authorities, the second is not, in general, though a few have supported small-scale experimental schemes.

Probably most health visitors today work on a model which lies somewhere between the two extremes outlined here. They recognize powerful societal forces which affect women's and children's health; but they also hold the view that mothers as individuals can do much to achieve better household health. So health visitors offer liaison, support and health education; liaison with housing and social security departments, support to help mothers cope better, and education to encourage them towards better health care practices.

Hearing mothers and health workers talking about their child-care work and their problems, suggests that both sets of people suffer from feelings of powerlessness, though both may also feel to some extent in a powerful position. Some mothers feel they control how money is spent within the household, and how they and their children spend the day. Some talk about their pleasure in bringing up their children as they wish, and their pride in having successfully reared their children. But mothers, as we have suggested, feel they cannot, in important and decisive respects, choose how to live their lives, and cannot without great difficulty improve household resources. In their care of themselves and of their children, they may feel especially helpless. We know that the mental health of women is at risk if they are at home full-time with small children, without adequate emotional support (e.g. Richman, 1976); evidence also suggests that their physical health may be affected (*see* Graham, 1984, Ch. 5). Less attention has been paid to possible damage to small children cooped up in small spaces full-time with their mothers; psychologists and policy-makers have been more concerned with potential damage if they are *not* with their mothers! (but *see* Richman, 1974). However, mothers will tell you of destructive, over-active, rebellious, bored and unhappy children, who are miraculously transformed when in the company of a wider range of people.

Most women lack the ability, as individuals, either to tackle their large-scale hindrances to a reasonable way of life, or fully to promote their children's health. Yet they may feel that most of the people they meet, and what they see and hear in the media, reinforce the assumption that they are in control and that they are accountable to society for their children's well-being.We think it is important that health workers and social workers do not take part in this reinforcement. This is perhaps especially important for workers who visit the home, since during this intervention, mothers may feel particularly vulnerable.

Our evidence suggests that health visitors and to some extent clinical medical officers also suffer from feelings of powerlessness. Both types of workers are required to carry out a formidable list of tasks, and this requirement may conflict with their perceptions of good practice. Thus doctors and health visitors said they could not always give enough time to each case. In another sense too they lacked power: to respond appropriately according to the needs of individuals. Thus even if they could find time to listen and discuss, they could not, in many cases, provide appropriate help.

However, both health visitors and doctors also wield some power in their work, and this was sometimes perceived by mothers as detrimental to their interests. Health workers could diagnose children as having certain problems and mothers as having certain orientations towards mothering. These views could be distressing immediately and could also acquire some permanence when enshrined in written records and reports, and other agencies: hospitals, social work and housing departments, the police, might be influenced by these opinions. We know that some health workers are concerned about problematic aspects of their own power, and one motive behind the current drive towards giving people access to their health records and giving parents children's health records to keep, is the desire to bring verdicts and opinions into the open.

We have suggested therefore that whether they like it or not, health workers, like other workers '*for*' people, such as social workers, exercise power over women as mothers. It can indeed be argued that, rather than recognizing that women have social problems, requiring societal solutions, we as a society encourage health and welfare staff to pathologize women's problems (Welburn, 1980). That is, we encourage them to diagnose individual women as functioning poorly or as sick. This kind of explanatory approach to women's problems itself may deepen popular belief, even among women themselves (paid and unpaid health workers) that their problems are indeed individual and that they themselves are to blame for not coping better.

In this respect it can further be argued that one function of health and welfare services is to control women, and it is women who are employed to do it (Brook and Davis, 1985). As a society, we put few resources such as financial support for mothers' work, day-care services, help with housing, into enabling women to live satisfactory lives. Instead women both paid and unpaid are encouraged to believe that it is a natural state of affairs for women to have to cope with poor resources and to become depressed when they cannot.

We think that one of the major problems for the women who provide health and welfare services is that while they may offer services with a benevolent motive, people may construe the service as motivated by the wish to control. We are in no doubt that, for instance, the health visitors we interviewed aimed to do good. A common and powerful theme in their accounts was the aim of working with mothers towards realization of the child's full potential. There is indeed, as Dingwall (1977) noted, an evangelical strand in health visitors' thinking. The conflict between benevolence and control has long been an issue in social work and in health care work. It is particularly where the work is interventionist that this conflict comes to the fore. For instance, when a health visitor visits with the benevolent intention of supporting and educating a mother, her visit on private territory can be perceived both by herself and the mother as a move towards assuming some power over activities in the home; this will be especially so if she takes the initiative in proposing and developing topics of conversation. Doctors in the preventive child health services avoid the problems because they offer a responsive rather than an interventionist service.

SOME THOUGHTS ON THE PREVENTIVE CHILD HEALTH SERVICES

Preventive child health services in Britain as currently structured and delivered are rooted in their history. Yet their characteristics are not inevitable or unchangeable. We have found the comparison of parental and health worker perspectives useful in helping us think about the services, as we have tried to show, and one of us (Marie-Claude Foster) has brought to our work valuable experience of services in other countries (in France and Africa); this too has helped cause us to look at our services from other standpoints (*see* also Foster, 1988a,b).

In brief, our services were developed to protect children, at a time when, while poverty was admitted as a cause of early death and ill-health, maternal ignorance was identified by some as both the root cause, and as the appropriate target for health service action (Lewis, 1980). Children's health and progress were to be regularly checked by doctors, and health visitors were to inspect homes and teach mothers hygiene and mothercraft. Service use by mothers has always been voluntary; again one can see the roots of this in the tradition of upholding parental rights (*see* Hewitt, 1958) and in particular in the Victorian debates over proposed compulsory immunization (Wohl, 1983). As service provision developed and a universalist approach was accepted, the home visit became enshrined as the means of reaching all mothers, and has been seen as essential, since some 'defaulters' did not come to the clinic. It has further been a continuing assumption of the services, as it has in social policy thinking in general about the family, that mothers, not fathers, care for children, and will be at home all the time – ready to be visited, and able to visit the clinic at times that suit staff.

As regards day-care for under-5s, too, the theme of protecting children has been at the root of our policies and practices. While other countries have expanded day-care, both to improve children's daily lives, and to encourage women to enter and stay in the labour force, the British view has been that the function of day-care is essentially preventive: to prevent breakdown of the family and reception of the child into care (*see* Riley, 1983; Tizard, Moss and Perry, 1976). There have been few measures to encourage women with children to engage in paid work.

We may note that the British understanding of 'protection' is idiosyncratic: it means confining children if possible to their mother's care. That is not the only possible definition. We would argue that children would be better protected if there were many more day-care places available for them. Currently, however, as in the past, mothers in Britain are held responsible for child-care, but the welfare state in the persons of its staff maintain surveillance through home visits. While service use is voluntary, staff see it as their task to promote it, in part so that surveillance may be maintained. Health services declare their interest in children's health and welfare not only by inspecting the child, but also by retaining records on the child's health and progress.

France provides an interesting alternative approach to preventive child health care (Foster, 1988a). It is well known for its pro-natalist policies. Policy makers believe that encouraging people to have children is a sensible policy for economic reasons and for military security. The state helps parents in a variety of practical ways. For example help is available with housing repayments for people with children; employment legislation takes family responsibilities into account, child benefits allocated to families are very generous by British standards (*see* for example Baker, 1986).

A second point is that in France the state acknowledges that parents, including mothers, have the right to continue in paid employment and to have time away from their children. There is an extensive provision of day-care facilities. Children start attending (often full time) day-care services at an early age – usually 3 months in day nurseries. Many 2 year olds are in nursery schools, and by the age of 3, 95% of children attend a nursery school (Kamerman and Kahn, 1980), many full time. The *haltes garderies* provide a useful service to parents not in paid work. They may leave their children for a few hours two or three times a week, while they shop, or whatever. There is also minding provision out of school hours.

In the field of health care the French state overtly says that parents as guardians of its future citizens must subject their children to a minimal level of medical surveillance, that is three compulsory medical examinations at approximately 8 days, 9 months and 2 years. These were until recently tied to child benefit payments but this is now no longer the case, possibly because take-up has become the norm. Certain vaccinations are compulsory for admission to school, that is polio, diphtheria and tetanus, and BCG is compulsory for any child being cared for in day-care centres. Parents hold their child's main medical records – the Carnet de Santé – which is given to them when they notify the child's birth.

Puéricultrices (state registered nurses who, like health visitors, have a further year's training) are employed both in day-care centres and in clinics. Those based in clinics work mainly *at* the clinic. They *offer* a home visit (after writing to parents to obtain their permission) to all parents with a new birth. Subsequently they carry out few home visits. They offer both health education and social activities to groups of parents. They provide an information and advice service at clinics, and appear to deal mainly with physical aspects of child health care. This is a service that responds to parents rather than intervenes.

It would be foolish to make firm statements about a system we have only glimpsed, but what we have noted about the French system does raise some interesting points which may cast light on ours.

The first point is that the package presented to parents seems both to offer certain goods as well as to require certain behaviours. Financial benefits and day-care services provide encouragement to parents to provide a good standard of living for their children. In return, as it were, parents are asked to bring their pre-school children for checks and immunizations at certain ages. From this side of the Channel, it seems that the state thus ascribes high value to the child-rearing work of parents and that the costs of children, and the welfare of children are seen as a shared responsibility between parents and state agencies.

Secondly, it seems that a merit of the system is that the division of responsibility between health agencies and parents is clearly demarcated and understood. Parents are responsible for maintaining the child's health: they keep the child record and are responsible for having the checks and immunizations carried out. Health staff offer a responsive service in that they are there at the clinic to examine the child when brought and to reply to questions. They limit their service mainly to the physical, rather than the social and moral. If health education is offered the programme of topics is one worked out and agreed between a group of parents and staff.

Thirdly, since most pre-school children, from an early age, spend some time each week in various forms of day-care, staff can keep a watchful eye on their well-being. Thus surveillance of children takes place in the public domain, in the normal course of the day.

Fourthly, it seems that in the French health care system duties are divided between paid workers in such a way that conflicts within the job are minimized. Thus the puéricultrice's job includes monitoring the child, and health education, with the emphasis on the physical development and care of the child. Other workers – psychologists and social workers – take on at an early stage cases of suspected maltreatment, under the aegis of the judiciary system, the 'juge d'enfants'. So 'policing' is separated out from community nursing and health education work.

Whether or not these two points are an entirely accurate representation of how services appear to French parents and staff, they may help us to think about the British system (See Mayall in press).

As we have suggested, the British approach to mothers includes calling them to account for their children's health and welfare, but does not include many measures to help them rear their children well. To us it seems that health visitors are unwitting agents who reinforce this unequal division of responsibility, since they are employed to help and encourage mothers to do better, within their existing resources and within a social framework which is not conducive to good child-rearing.

Secondly, it seems to us that the division of responsibility between mothers and health and welfare staff is not clearly stated and agreed between the two sides. For instance, mothers may think it is up to them when and whether to use services, but may be harrassed by health visitors who think they are responsible for ensuring high take-up. Health visitors think they should educate mothers, but do not say so clearly, and mothers may reject covert or explicit educational ploys. Mothers who use registered minders may think the local authority who registers the minder is responsible for standards of care; but mothers get blamed for 'dumping' their children with bad minders (even if registered).

Some pioneering work has been done in Britain to redefine and reallocate responsibility for health care. We noted earlier that in Oxfordshire child health care records are held by parents. In the area of antenatal care, a policy has been adopted in Newbury (Berkshire) of women holding their own obstetric records. They did not lose them! Also their satisfaction and well-being increased: they felt more in control of their care, and found it easier to talk with staff (Elbourne *et al.*, 1987).

Thirdly, it is interesting and provocative that French medical and nursing staff appear to limit their field of interest mainly to the physical and developmental health of the child. While it may be difficult to separate these aspects entirely from social and moral aspects of health and health care, the attempt to do so does seem worth considering. Health visitors in particular might consider this point. It is at least questionable whether health staff should intervene in parental goals.

Fourthly, we note that the French system for overseeing children's well-being seems more efficient and less intrusive than the British system of home visiting. The fact that this overseeing work is done by day-care staff and taken up in case of suspected problems by social workers, means that health care workers do not have conflicting roles, as British health visitors do (*see* Chapter 4), as health educators, supporters and inspectors.

SOME THOUGHTS ON FUTURE DIRECTIONS

At this point we should say that we do not see it as part of our remit to offer prescriptions of any kind for the future. That would be presumptuous. For us this is both an exciting and a difficult time to be writing this last chapter (September 1988). There have in recent years been important reports on the primary and preventive health services (Royal College of General Practitioners, 1982; DHSS, 1986a,b; HMSO, 1987). We know there are many changes both taking place and being considered by those concerned with providing the preventive child health services. As ever though, there is a good deal of talk about 'increasing consumer participation' and 'parental involvement', there has been very little consideration given to taking parental perspectives seriously. We have tried to give some expression to these here and elsewhere (Mayall, 1986).

Here, finally, are some very general notes on possible future directions for preventive child health services within the present social framework. But first, though we are being tentative, we would like to go back to those two phrases about 'increasing consumer participation' and 'parental involvement'; we would like firmly to reiterate that people do not consume health or health services! They make and maintain their own health with a little help sometimes – and a lot occasionally – from the health services! Women also work for the health of their small children, and (often) of their partners (*see* Stacey, 1976, 1988; Graham, 1984). It is inappropriate to talk about increasing 'parental involvement', except that it would be good to see large-scale tax and employment measures to increase *paternal* involvement. In Britain it is mothers who do almost all the child-care, and they are fully involved. They radically alter their lives to give good care, and receive little recognition for that reorganization. Notably most mothers subordinate to this child-care priority paid work and careers, over periods of up to 20 years and, as Joshi (1987) points out, their earnings over a life-time suffer drastically as a consequence. It is not more involvement from mothers that is needed, but more involvement from day-care and education services, town-planners, public transport agencies and shop-owners, to make life with children pleasanter, and to give practical and symbolic recognition to their importance in our society.

As regards the preventive health services, we would suggest that the emphasis given by health staff to mothers and their under–5s is misplaced nowadays. By comparison with the situation 50 or 100 years ago, women are well educated; they are able to acquire and weigh up knowledge and advice from a wide variety of sources, including friends and relatives, books and magazines. They are highly motivated and will seek help if and when they need it from health staff, and are also willing to use services if requested to do so. (It would help if employers recognized parental need for paid time off to use services.) This is not to say that health care work with and for mothers and under-5s is unimportant, but that the priority and time allotted to it might usefully be judged in the context of other groups' health care needs.

We would like to see a clinic-based service for parents and children, with clear guidelines issued to all parents about when they should (minimally) bring their children, and why. Parents should hold their child's health records, and should be asked to produce them as evidence of service use when the child starts primary school (c.f. National Children's Bureau, 1987). Home visits could be offered for new babies and would take place only if mothers accepted the offer and, for older children, if they requested a visit.

We favour the broad model for services proposed by Cumberlege (DHSS, 1986b): a service which focuses on the neighbourhood. It would be staffed by a team of nurses and doctors, dentists and chiropodists (as many are at present). It would both seek to identify local health issues and problems and aim to help people maintain and improve their health. It would offer a clinic-based service which would offer both individual and group sessions. People would come for screening and advice on an individual basis. Group work might include identification of staff with local people, of their perceived problems and joint discussion in order to work towards greater knowledge on both sides, and to identify possible courses of action.

In essence we are arguing that preventive health service staff might think of their work in the context of public health issues, and could work towards consideration of how their own particular skills can best be used in that context. We suggest that they work together with other agencies such as local planning and social service departments, health promotion units and environmental health departments, to study local people's perspectives on health problems, health issues and health service needs; and to plan services which are responsive to local wishes and where the many skills available among the District Health Authority and local authority are well deployed.

To us it seems clear that to provide such services requires staff both to focus on geographical areas and to work together in teams. Health centres and clinics with defined catchment areas and a range of staff skills are well placed to do this. General practitioners who work in ones and twos are much less well placed to carry out preventive work, and evidence over the years suggests that in spite of attempts by the medical establishment to promote their increased participation in preventive child health work, GPs themselves have not (on the whole) responded with enthusiasm (National Children's Bureau, 1987).

For too long the preventive child health services have been on the defensive *and* embattled. We know that both clinical medical officers and health visitors have felt their work and their very existence to be under threat, over the years, from various pressures. For instance, there has been a long skirmishing war among doctors: GPs on one side, community paediatricians on another and clinical medical officers on yet another, have debated who should do preventive work with children. Health visitors have felt under threat as managers have urged them to justify their pay-cheques, in terms of effectiveness. The services have always been poorly resourced and quality has suffered in consequence.

We think there is scope for up-grading the image of preventive health by redesigning services to cover local populations; possibly they might then attract a larger share of DHA budgets. But, even without that, re-organization and re-focusing of targets could lead to more efficient and effective use of staff time.

There is a whole new world of work out there for community health service staff, with plenty of challenging and satisfying work to do. In the current political climate we hear a good deal of rhetoric about the community, community care, and the importance of people taking responsibility for their own health. Like any slogans, they may be used to justify policies and practices that do not suit us all, but perhaps we can seize upon them and use them to our own advantage. These are the bandwagons for community health service staff to jump on, and we wish them *bon voyage*! Meanwhile mothers can be trusted to care for their children.

APPENDIX 1
PERSPECTIVES ON CHILD-CARE: PARENTS AND HEALTH VISITORS

(A BRIEF SUMMARY OF THE DESIGN AND METHOD)

This study was funded by the Economic and Social Research Council (1985–1988) and carried out at the Thomas Coram Research Unit (41 Brunswick Square, London WC1N 1AZ). Fieldwork took place in 1986.

The aim of the study was to explore the perspectives, mainly of mothers and health visitors, on good child-care. We aimed to focus on a sample of households which reflected the social and ethnic diversity of the population with which health visitors work. The sample was limited to those with a first child aged 21 months when first interviewed. In order to explore people's perspectives fully, we planned to focus on small samples.

The study was based initially in one District Health Authority (DHA) area in London, where the households lived and the health visitors worked. The area was socially and ethnically diverse, with up to one-third of under-5s other than white indigenous.

In order to obtain a small multi-ethnic sample we adopted the following procedure: DHA staff used their computer records to identify all households with first children of the appropriate age (159). They then sought permission from the parents for us to approach them. Nineteen refused or had moved away. We then called at the 140 remaining addresses. Seven refused and 24 had moved or were unobtainable (after five visits). We carried out a 10-minute screening interview, covering demographic data and service use, with the remaining 109 and from these selected households for the main sample. The method here was: we stratified the addresses by geographical area, listed them randomly and approached them in list order.

We aimed for a sample of about 30, where about one-quarter of mothers were white (in our view) and born in the UK, and three quarters did not meet at least one of these two criteria. In the event we had a sample of 33 households – diverse, both socially and ethnically, and weighted towards ethnic minority status (*see* Table 1.1, pp. 6–7).

It was crucial to obtain the main caregiver's permission (usually the mother) and on this basis we included the household in the study. We then asked fathers (if available) to take part. Twelve of the 24 agreed. Mothers were interviewed three times (twice in six cases at monthly intervals; fathers once).

The London health visitor sample was, again, stratified by area, and by other factors: full-time versus part-time, field-worker versus team-leader, generic versus specialist. Of the 30 health visitors selected, two refused. The sample was about one-half of the health visitors working for the DHA. Health visitors were interviewed three times at monthly interviews.

In addition, time permitted us to extend the study to include all the clinical medical officers who worked regularly for the DHA (11); they were interviewed once.

We also decided to broaden the study to include, for comparison, a sample of health visitors working in a different area: a county area outside London. The sample procedure was as before, and the sample of 20 was one-quarter of all the health visitors in the DHA.

In all:

	n
screen interviews	109
main sample mothers	33
main sample fathers	12
London health visitors	28
London clinical medical officers	11
County health visitors	20

APPENDIX 2
INTERVIEW SCHEDULES

HEALTH VISITORS: FIRST INTERVIEW

1 Caseload

(a) Can you tell me your pattern of work – are you GP-attached or working from a geographical area?

(b) Can you tell me a bit about your caseload and your area?
> *Prompts*
> GP-attachment/geographical
> Age distribution

What are the general characteristics of your patch – as regards, housing, roads, parks, other amenities?

Is there much unemployment among men, among women?

(c) Can we now concentrate on your families with under-5s?
> *Prompts*
> What kind of class and ethnic mix do you have?
> What kinds of housing do they live in?
> Is there much mobility?
> Do you have any families new to this country?

2 Working Conditions

(a) *How easy* do you find it to do your work as an employee of this authority?
> *Prompts*
> Staffing level
> Help with clerical work (administration)
> Office space
> Travelling

(b) (Given the constraints you've mentioned) Do you have enough *control* over work?

Prompts

> Do you have to report back to anyone and for what (e.g.
> employing authority, manager, other professionals)?
> To what extent do you decide your own priorities?
> To what extent do you decide on the structure of your
> working week?

(c) Do you find you get enough support in your work?

3A *Home visits*

(a) How do you feel about offering your services to households with
young children — knocking on a door and saying 'I'm your health
visitor?'

3B *Recent home visit*
(NB if no recent visit, ask again at 2nd, 3rd interview)

(a) Can you think about your *most* recent visit to a household with a
child age 21 months (preferably one where the child was the
focus of the visit; visit lasted more than 5 minutes no more than 2
weeks ago).
Can you tell me about that visit?

(b) *Prompts*
> Why did you go?
> Who initiated the visit?
> What happened?
> What did you aim to do?
> Was it successful?
> What do you think were the parents' concerns (anything else)?

(c) Were there some topics you wanted to raise? Why? Did you raise
all of them? Why/why not?

(d) Did you feel happy about child-care in that household?
Do they give good care?
What makes you say that?
What are the good points about the parents' care?
Are there any bad points? What are they?

(e) Was there anything you thought the parents did not know but that
they needed to know — did you think you should tell them about
it?

(f) Was the child healthy?
What makes you say that?
(g) What do you think the parents thought you came for?
(h) Do you and the parent(s) agree about good health care for young children? If not, what happens?

4 Health care of under-2s

Can I go on to ask you a bit more about the health care of young children? We're interested in children around the age of 21 months.
(a) Can you think of a really healthy child you know, of that age? Can you describe that child?
(b) What do you think brings about good health in a young child?
(c) With a child of that age (21 months) are there some health care *practices* which you think are important for keeping the child healthy? Why?
(d) Do you raise/discuss these topics with the parents? Why?

5 Two child-rearing topics: food and social contacts

Can we take a couple of specific topics to do with child-rearing (as regards children aged 21 months or so).
Food
(a) How important do you think food is? And why?
(b) What do you think are good practices on food for this age-group?
(c) Do some of the parents need help on nutrition for their children (i.e. according to health visitor's criteria of good practices)?
(d) Do some of the parents have difficulties giving good care (according to health visitor's criteria)? Why?
(e) Do you try to introduce this topic, routinely, for this age-group?

6 Contacts with other children
Same set of questions 5 (a) to (e) above.

7 Child welfare: three topics

Can I ask you your ideas on some specific points to do with children's welfare?
(a) Some children eat a lot of *sweets* and sugary things. How do you account for that?

(b) I expect you know that children in working class households (especially in class V) are more likely than other children to have accidents.
Why do you think that is?

(c) *Child abuse*
There's been a lot of talk recently about child abuse.
What do you think causes some parents to injure their children?
What do you see as your role with regard to child abuse?

HEALTH VISITORS: SECOND INTERVIEW

8 *Health visiting tasks*

(a) We know you carry out a lot of different tasks/jobs as a HV. We'd like to discuss later on different ways of working. But can we first talk about three of the basic jobs.

- clinic sessions
- home visits
- developmental checks

Prompts for each
Do you think that service is important? Why?
Do you think parents value it? Why?

(b) Do you think the local child preventive health services are good — in your patch/your practice?

(c) Can you say anything about the quality of the services more widely across the District?

(d) How do you see the clinical medical officer's (CMO's) role in the services?

9 *Immunization*

(a) Can you tell me about the most recent occasion when the subject of immunization came up (i.e. as a discussion topic)?
Prompts
Can you tell me what happened?
Who said what/who raised what topic?
What did you see as your role?
How do you think the parent(s) perceived your role?

(b) In general how do you see your role as regards immunization?
(c) Why do you think parents have immunizations done and why do they not have it done?

10 *Parental need for help*

(a) Do you think parents need help from professionals with preventive child health care?
(b) Who needs it (is that everyone)?
What do they need?
Why do they need it?
(c) Do you think parents should use the services offered?
(d) What kinds of help do they ask you for?
Can you give it?

11 *Models of child care*

(a) At a general level, thinking of the parents with under-2s on your case-load, are there some who have different ideas from you about good health care for young children?
What are these differences?
(b) How do you account for them?
(c) How do you see your role in such circumstances?

12 *Parental problems*

(a) Thinking about it from a parental view, what do you think are the main problems parents face in bringing up their children (under-2s) healthily?
(b) Do you see it as your job to try to help with that? (each problem)
(c) Of the problems you do see it as your job to help with:
Which aspects/problems can you help with (or health staff)?
And which can't you help with and why?

13 *Difficulties with some households*

And are there some households/parents where you feel you have

particular difficulties in doing your job as you would like?
Can you tell me more about them?
What do you do then?

14 *Priorities*

(a) Are there some households you think you should concentrate on? Which and why? What are your aims?
(b) How do you think these parents perceive you? (Get two examples)

15 *Working week*

Can you tell me about your working week, last/most recent week?
> *Prompts*
> What did you most want to do? Did you manage it?
> What were the most satisfying parts of the week?
> And the least satisfying?
> Would you say you had some/any successes?
> And any failures?

Remember to ask for the list

List of children aged 21 months (or 20, 22 months if necessary) for third interview (Q. 16).

HEALTH VISITORS: THIRD INTERVIEW

16 *Case study* of one household, with a first 21 month old picked at random from each health visitor's list.

(a) Can you tell me about this household?
> How many people live there?
> How are they related?
> Employment/unemployment if known.
> Who looks after the children?

How long have you known them?

How often have you been in contact? Why? If not, why not?

(b) What are your health visiting objectives with this household?

What do you think are the 'health needs' of this household?

How can you identify any health needs?

What can be done about these?

(c) What do you think are the parents' priorities for the child-care of this child (21 month old)?

(d) Does this household provide good health care for child/children?

Prompts

Why is that?

Is it easy for them to give good care?

(e) If there are any problems/difficulties in the family, why is that?

(f) What is it that *you* can contribute to their health, that no one else can?

17 *Motherhood*

(a) On the whole, it seems to be mothers mainly who care for under-5s. Do you think that's the best arrangement?

(b) Is it a difficult job?

Is it a job people can do by instinct/naturally?

(c) Professionals often say/you've mentioned that some mothers seem depressed/low, and studies show high rates of depression in some groups of mothers.

Why do you think mothers of young children get depressed?

(d) If you take a woman with a socially important job like being a doctor, social worker, health visitor, maths teacher:

How do you rate in importance being a full-time mother in comparison?

Prompt

Is it a worthwhile use of adult time?

(e) As an HV do you think it would be useful to see more fathers? Why?

18 *Ethnic minorities*

(a) Do you think that health visiting in this area has responded to the fact that we are now a multi-ethnic society?

What else do you think health visiting could do (to give a good response)?
(b) What do you think people from various ethnic minorities think about health visiting?
(c) Here you are working in a multi-ethnic society. Do you think your colour affects how people treat you?
(d) And how you deliver the services?

19 Unemployment

(a) Would you say that unemployment among local people has had any effect on your work?
(b) And if unemployment continues at the present rate, or only slightly lower, do you think such a future has implications for the work of health visitors?

20 Work in unequal society

You work in an area with some very wealthy and some very poor people, and nationally it looks as if children have unequal chances of health. How do you see your role/work in these circumstances?

21 Are there other appropriate ways of doing health visiting in our society? Are you involved in any of these?

22 Contacts

(a) Do you have any contact as a health visitor with any groups outside the NHS – for instance women's health groups, black groups, community groups?
(b) Has it altered your perspectives on your work?

23 This study

You know what this study is about. And we've asked you a lot of questions.
Are there other issues that you think we should be discussing?

Background data

Could I ask you a few questions about yourself. Could you tell me:

1 When were you born   month .... year ....

2 Where were you born ....? And your parents ....?
   And brought up ....

3 Can you tell me what sort of work your father and mother did/do
   Father's main job ....   (RG)
   Mother's main job ....

4 And what school leaving qualifications did you   CSE ....
   get (Public exams)   O ....
                                         A ....

   Did you have any other qualifications or training apart from SRN
   and HV?

5 Could you tell me about your career to date: training, jobs, time
   spent in child-bearing and child-care

dates	*training/occupation*
....	....
....	....
....	....

6 (a) Then can I ask you where you trained to be a health visitor?
   ....

   (b) And you've been a health visitor for .... years, altogether?

   (c) And in this area (DHA) how long have you worked as a health
   visitor?   .... years

7 (a) In-service training, continuing education of any kind,
   refresher courses, have you been on anything of this kind?

   (b) Did your HV training equip you for the job in practice?
   What improvements would you suggest?
   Do you intend to stay in health visiting? Do you have other career
   plans or wishes?

8 Can you tell me where you live?
   DHA
   Outside London.

9 Do you have any children?
   If health visitor has children:
   How many do you have?
   How old are they?
   Do you have to make any arrangements to have them cared for
   while you work?

Or have you had to in the past?
10 Do you work full-time or part-time?
No. of hours a week worked ....
11 And you work from the clinic? .... attached to a GP ....?
If attached: is that in all parts of the GP's area or some areas only
and as well as that do you cover a patch?
12 *If attached to a GP*:
(a) How many doctors do you work with?
(b) And how many practices?

MOTHER INTERVIEWS

*During the course of three interviews, carried out at monthly (?)
intervals, data should be collected on the following topics.*

*At each interview cover: accounts of the most recent encounter
with preventive health service staff and recent history of household
events, illness, crises.*

*Otherwise data can be collected in accordance with parental
priorities. A suggested order is given below.*

First interview

1 Child's day yesterday.
2 Life with x in this housing, this area.
3 Child-care now compared to 6 months ago.
4 Health status – child and parents.
5 Recent encounters with health professionals – health visitor,
clinic doctor, other preventive service.

Second interview

6 Recent health, illness, events in household – effects on child-care.
7 Lay and professional network.
Health care of self; satisfaction with social network re self and
media.
8 Decisions on immunization.
9 Development checks: recent experience.
0 As 5 above.

Third interview

11 As 6 above.
12 Preventive services for children locally: knowledge, accept ability, usefulness.
13 Child health care at home – detail.
14 Demographic data.
15 As 5 above.

Introduction to parents

Cover the following points early on in the interview.

We are from an independent research unit.
  We have no connection with the NHS.
  We have permission to do this study from the District Health Authority.
    We found the names and addresses of households from clinic lists
    We chose the families randomly.
      All the data is confidential, that is, we never reveal names or give information to anyone that could serve to identify people. Instead we use the information we collect to describe what groups of people say. For instance, how many people think this, or have had this sort of experience.
        This study is concerned to find out what parents think about child-care and about health services in the area. We are also going to find out what the people who provide services think is good child care and what they think about the services. We aim to see if the two sets of people have the same sorts of ideas.
          The purpose of the study is to consider whether health services meet parents' needs and wishes; and to suggest ways in which the services can be developed so they suit parents of young children.
            There are two of us doing the study. Both of us are mothers. Both have a lot of practical knowledge on bringing up children.

MOTHERS: FIRST INTERVIEW

1 *Child's day yesterday*

Can you tell me about your day yesterday from first thing (when you got up) to last thing. Then can you tell me a bit more about how x spent the day.

> *Prompts*
>> *Make sure you cover:*
>>> all food – meals and snacks
>>> activities – play, outings
>>> people present with x (visitors to home, meetings with others)
>>> rests/sleep
>>> *cleaning* her up (washing, nappies, toilet training, teeth).

(a) Did she have a good day – what was good about it?
    Were there any difficulties for you in giving x a good day?
(b) And was there anything about the day that was bad for x?
(c) Were there things you usually do that you didn't do?
    Why was that?
(d) And is there anything you would like to do for x, that you can't do?
    Is there anything you would like for x that is impossible or difficult?
    Why is that?
(e) Did you do anything yesterday on purpose to keep x healthy?

Research questions
(a) *What do people think is good for children (including good for health)?*
(b) *What is the domestic/local context of child-care (constraints and opportunities)?*

2 Life with x in this housing, this area

(a) Can you tell me what it is like (how you feel about) bringing up your child round here?
    > *Prompts*
    >> For *housing* and *neighbourhood* ask:
    >> Are you happy with your housing/neighbourhood, for bringing up x ?
    >> What are the good points?
    >> Any bad points?
    >> If *satisfied*: is there anything else you would prefer?
    >> If *dissatisfied*: what is your idea of good housing/neighbourhood for bringing up children?
(b) Can I ask you (some more) about keeping x safe?
    (i) Do you think this is a fairly safe flat/house for x to live?
        So are there any risk to x's safety here?

And in the neighbourhood?
  (ii) For each type of risk mentioned ask
       What do you do about it?
 (iii) What is it like keeping x safe, now she's older? (Is it easier or
       more difficult?)
       Why is that?
  (iv) *If not mentioned*: what about your flat/house – are there
       things about it that are dangerous, but you can't do anything
       about them? Can you tell me about that?
       What about the neighbourhood?
       Make sure you cover:
         falls/collisions
         burns and scalds
         electricity
         drowning in bath
         swallowing things (poison, objects)
         road dangers
(c) Do you feel you and x are living your lives the way you want to?
     Prompt
       Is there anything you would like to be different?
       Are there any difficulties?
(d) Is it an easy area to live in?
    Are people pleasant, friendly, helpful?
     Prompt
       Your neighbours.
       People in the street, at the shops.
       At the doctor's.
       At the clinic.

Research questions
(a) *What are parental perceptions of good health care, and good safety care?*
(b) *What do they perceive as environmental constraints?*

3 Child health care now compared to 6 months ago

Can I ask you what it's like looking after x *now* compared to 6 months
ago (when she was . . . months old)?
Prompts
    What is x's day like now compared to then?
    Why is/are there that/those difference/s?

Now she's older, does that make a difference to how you look after her?

What are these differences? Why do you care for her in different ways?

And how do you feel about being a parent now? Is it enjoyable? Is it easier, more difficult?

Do you feel you've changed (as a parent) since x was born? How?

Research questions

(a) *What do parents perceive as important child-care jobs 'now' and why?*

(b) *What kinds of knowledge do they have about their children?*

(c) *Knowledge and skills parents have and perceive as important.*

4 Health status

(a) *Concepts of optimal health*

(i) *Child health*

(a) Could you think about a really healthy child of this age, and describe her or him?

(b) What do you think brings about really good health in a young child?

(c) Can you give her everything she needs to keep her healthy?
   If not: Why is that?
   Prompts
   Some people say they have difficulties caring for their children because of their housing, family relationships, money problems, work or not work problems, illness of family members. Has there been anything like that (in the last month?) that has made caring for x difficult?
   (ii) Then can you think about *adult health.*

(d) How would you describe a really healthy adult?

(e) Are you really healthy yourself?

(f) What brings about good health in an adult?

(g) Can you do/manage all these things at present?

(b) *Can I ask you now about your child's health?*
   Could I start with two general questions (i.e. the General Household Survey health questions)
   (i) Does x have any long-standing disability or infirmity?
   By long-standing I mean anything that has troubled her/him

over a period of time or that is likely to affect her/him over a period of time?
If yes:
What is the matter with x?
Does this illness or disability limit x's activities in any way?
(ii)   Now could you think about the 2 weeks ending yesterday. During those two weeks, did x have to cut down on any of the things s/he usually does because of (disability as in (i) or some other) illness or injury?
If yes: How many days in all was this during these 2 weeks?

(c)   *Health history*
Can I ask you about any illnesses x has had/? Can I list some of the illnesses children have and ask if she's had any of them?
Did she have any health problems when she was first born, or in the early months?
Has she had any serious health problem, or has she any sort of handicap?
Has she had any of these illnesses:

measles	Yes	No
mumps	Yes	No
German measles	Yes	No
scarlet fever	Yes	No
whooping cough	Yes	No
chicken pox	Yes	No

Has she ever had any convulsions or fits or turns?
Prompts
How many times?
When were they?
What did you think it was? Did you talk to anyone about it?
Did you get any professional advice or help?
Did a doctor or a health visitor give a diagnosis/say what it was?
What treatment did you give? Did you suggest that?
What do you think about it now (are you worried, concerned)?
Has she ever had *earache* lasting more than 24 hours, a discharging ear or an ear infection?
Prompts
As above.
Or bronchitis, asthma or wheezing?
Prompts
As above.

Eczema?
Prompts
  As above.
And has she had any other serious illness (one that has worried you or others)?

(d) *Current health status*
  (i) And more recently, if you think about the last 4 weeks, how has x been?
    Prompt
      Have you had any worries about her health?
      Has she had anything wrong?
      For all worries and illness episodes ask:
      How long did it last?
      What did you do about it?
      Whom did you talk to? How useful were they?
      Was it easy to care for x? Problems?
  (ii) Do you think x is healthy at present/nowadays?
    Prompt
      Compared to other children, is she more or less likely to get illnesses? Why is that?
  (iii) Do you usually/routinely do anything to stop her getting ill? What and why?
  (iv) How about for yourself? Do you do anything to stop yourself getting ill? What and why? And for (others in household)?
    If different or no preventive measures done for self, ask: Why do you do those things for x and not for yourself?

(e) *Progress*
Over the last 6 months, has she changed/progressed/learned to do new things?
Prompts
  Do you think she's progressing well? How do you know?
  Are you worried about her at all – her progress, her behaviour?
  Why is that? Have you done anything about it? Talked to anyone? Was that helpful?
Research questions
(a) *What do parents perceive to be good health in children and how do they think children acquire good health?*

(b) What are the household's opportunities and constraints for giving good care?

(c) Do parents have models of good progress in children?

(d) Whom do they consult and find useful?

(f) Can I ask you about your health?
Again (as for x) some general questions to start with *(GHS)*:
   (i)   Over the last 12 months, would you say your health has been
         good
         fairly good
         or not good?
   (ii) Do you have any long-standing illness, disability or infirmity?
         By long-standing I mean anything that has troubled you over
         a period of time or that is likely to trouble you over a period of
         time.
         If yes:
         What is the matter with you?
         Does this illness or disability limit your activities in any
         way?
   (iii) Could you think about the 2 weeks ending yesterday.
         During those 2 weeks did you have to cut down on any of the
         things you usually do (about the house/at work or in your free
         time) because of disability (as in (ii) above) or some other
         illness or injury?
         If yes: How many days was this in all during these 2 weeks?

(g) Then can you look back at the last 4 weeks? How have you all
been?
For any household member's health problems ask:
   Can you tell me about that?
   How long did it last?
   Any discussion within household?
   Any help sought outside household – lay and professional?
   Did it make a difference to x, or to how you cared for x?

(h) And has anything else happened lately – that has made a
difference to x – how she spends her time, her health, how she is
cared for?
   Prompts
      Any changes or problems to do with, for instance housing,
      work, income, day-care, relatives (illness, crises).

And how has that affected you?

Research questions

(a) *How far are health problems, other problems resolved within household? To whom outside household do people turn?*

(b) *What are relationships between child health care and child health and other events, health problems in household?*

5 Recent encounters with health professionals for preventive health care

Note   This question to be asked at all three parents' interviews

(a) Can I ask you if you have talked with anyone like a health visitor, a doctor at the clinic, or a nurse about x recently (during the last 4 weeks)?

Cover all contacts in last month for prevention, assessment, pro-active care including hospital, GP, clinic, home visits.

   Prompts

   Can you tell me what happened?

   Did you go/ask for a visit, or did they ask you to go/visit you?

   Why did you go?

   What do you think the (HV, Dr, etc) came for/wanted to do, say?

   Were there some topics you wanted to raise?

   Did you have enough time to discuss/talk about it/the problem etc?

   Do you think they respected your views/listened to you/took what you said seriously?

   How did you get on with the HV, Dr, etc?

   Were you happy about the meeting?

(b) *Health visitor*

   What topics does the health visitor most want to talk about/seem most eager to raise?

   Has the health visitor ever raised the topic of/talked to you about:
      safety
      play/toys/stimulation
      food
      toilet-training?

   What do you think are her views on (each of these)?

What do you think about her views?
Why do you think she comes?

Research questions
(a) *Why do parents contact NHS preventive services?*
(b) *How useful are the services?*
(c) *What do parents perceive to be the character (purposes, assumptions) of NHS preventive services? Are these acceptable?*

MOTHERS: SECOND INTERVIEW

6 *Recent health, illness, events in household – and effects or child-care*

(a) Can I ask you how everyone in the household has been lately?
Have you all been *well* (over last 4 weeks)?
For any household member's health problem
Can you tell me about that?
When was it?
How long did it last?
What did you/they do about it?
Any discussion within household?
Any help sought outside household – lay and professional?
Did it make a difference to x or to how you cared for x?

(b) And has anything else happened lately – that has made
difference to x – how she spends her time, her health, how she
cared for?
Prompts
Any changes or problems to do with, for instance, housing
work, income, day-care, relatives (illness, crises).
And how has that affected you?

Research questions
(a) How far are health problems, other problems resolved within
household? To whom outside household do people turn?
(b) What are relationships between child health care and child heal
and other events, health problems in household?

7 Lay and professional networks

We're trying to find out with whom people talk about their children, so can I ask you:

(a) Do you enjoy talking about x?
And do you feel you need to talk about her?
So with whom do you mainly talk? . . . And anyone else?
   Prompts
      What about on the phone?
      Do you meet with people in any sort of group and talk about children then?
   Thinking about last week – what topics came up to do with x?
   Did you enjoy talking about that/her?
   Was it helpful to talk about it?

(b) And again, thinking back, can you think about the last time you had a problem in caring for x, or had to make a decision how to care for her . . .?
Can you tell me about that?
   Prompts
      Again, did you talk about it with anyone? (lay or professional)
      Who was that?
      Was it helpful?

(c) *If not mentioned so far, and in any case make sure you cover:*
Do you find health visitors, doctors, any other person at the clinic, surgery, hospitals useful to talk with about x?
   Prompts
      Can you tell me about any time when you had a useful talk with anyone like that? What was good about it?
      And have there been times when you have asked for help and not got it? Can you tell me about that?

(d) So altogether, do you feel you have enough people to turn to/around:
      – when you want to chat about x?
      – when you feel you *need* to talk about her?
   Are there people you would like to talk with, but they aren't here, around (live elsewhere etc.)?

(e) *Circles*
(*Focus of this is who are the important* people as regards help/talk *re x.*)

We're trying to find out who are the important people parents turn to about their children, who is useful, gives good advice, is reliable.

So could you look at this chart (Fig. 1) and think about the people you talk with . . . including relatives, friends, doctors, health visitor, anyone else.

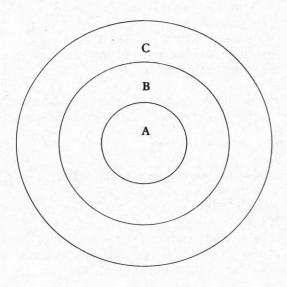

Fig. 1 People you talk with about your child:

A. People you trust, you value their advice and views.
B. People you might talk with and like to hear their views.
C. People whose views you don't value highly. And people who offer advice unasked.

Note. Thanks to Yvonne Dhouge for her help. (See also Walman 1984).

(f) (i) How about yourself? If you have any worries about yourself or any health problems – who do you talk to?
   Prompt
   In the household (your husband/x's father)?
   Relatives, friends?
   Anyone else?

(ii) Last time you were worried about yourself (upset, anxious, ill) or had to make a decision, with whom did you talk? Anyone else?

Prompt

Was that helpful?

(iii) Do you feel you have enough people to talk with if you are worried, concerned, ill?

Prompt

What about your husband/x's father – do you talk with him?

Are there people you miss/are cut off from (e.g. live in another area, place)?

Research questions

(a) *Do parents need help with child-care? To whom do they turn and for what?*

(b) *Do they perceive NHS staff as useful sources of help and for what?*

(c) *Do parents feel well supported as regards their own health and other problems?*

(g) *Media*

We're trying to find out if people find TV or papers or books useful and interesting in caring for their children.

(i) If we take yesterday did you see, or hear or read anything about children or child-care that you found interesting?

Prompt

TV, radio

magazines, newspapers

leaflets, books.

(ii) Do you find any of these say useful or interesting things about caring for children: TV, papers, magazines, leaflets, books? Can you give an example (topic + media)?

(iii) Do you have any child-care books?

What are they?

Do you find you turn to them for information or for help?

(iv) If you take a recent time when you had to make a decision about x on caring for her:

Cover

feeding her

keeping her safe

dental care.

Did you get? any information from the media (TV, books, papers etc)?
Was it useful?
Did it affect what you did?

8 *Immunization*

Could we talk about immunization?
Can I ask you what you did about immunization for x?
   Prompts
      Which ones did you have done?
      Why did you decide *for* those?
      And why did you *not* have those/the others done?
      Did you talk with anyone about it?
      What did they say? Was it useful, helpful?
      Did you find out about immunization in any other way (leaflets, books, TV, what happened to anyone you knew)?
      Did you take the decisions yourself? Or did anyone else take decisions or help you decide (share responsibility)?
      Were you happy with that?
      Was there anything that made it difficult to get the immunization done (child or adult illness, getting to the clinic, moving house, holidays, no reminders)?

Note what immunizations done

DPT	one	two	three shots
DT	one	two	three shots
Polio	one	two	three shots
Measles		yes	no

Research questions
(a) *How helpful are lay networks, other sources of information and NHS staff in helping parents decide about immunization?*
(b) *Who takes responsibility for immunization and how far do parents think responsibility rests with them?*

9 *Developmental checks*

I expect you know that in this area the clinic or the doctor will

check your baby for you at various ages.
Can I ask you about that?

(a) Has x been seen/had any of these checks
    at 6 weeks
    6–8 months
    18 months?

(b) Could you tell me about the most recent check you had done?
    Why did you have it done?
        Prompts
        What happened?
        What was it for/what was it testing?
        Did they do it well?
        What was it like for x?
        How did you feel about it?
        Did you want to talk about anything – how did that go? Did
            you have time to do that?

(c) Have you found the checks valuable?
        Prompts
        Do you think they are good tests?
        Do the HVs/Drs do them well?
        Have you learned anything/do you find it helpful/useful?
        Are you happy to have x looked at, or tested?
        Why do you think they do them?
Research questions
(a) *Do parents perceive child assessment by NHS staff as competent
    and valuable?*

*10 Recent encounters with health professionals for preventive
health care*

As in Question 5

Health care topics

(a) *Some parents have told us about kinds of care they think are
    important.*

Can I ask you what you think about them?
> *Cover*
>> dental care
>> hygiene
>> warmth.
> *And for each ask*
>> Do you think that matters for health?
>> Do you do anything about that?
>> What about yesterday/when was the most recent time?
>> *If it is seen as important*: Do you find it easy to do that?
>> Any problems yesterday/most recent time?
>> Are there any things that make it difficult including that (e.g. housing, neighbourhood, transport, adults' work)?
>> Have you talked with anyone about that, or read about it or asked for information or help?

Food yesterday

(b) Finally, can I ask you to tell me about what your child ate all day yesterday. *Fill in chart below.*
> *Prompts*
>> Do you think food matters for her health?
>> What is it you are aiming to do/How will it help?
>> Do you find it easy to give good food? For instance what about yesterday?
>> Are there any things that make it difficult (e.g. housing, neighbourhood, money, transport, adults' work, child's preferences)?
>> Have you talked to anyone about it or read about it or asked for information or help?

Appendix 2

Food and drink yesterday

From child's waking up time yesterday to waking up time today.

Time	Food and drink (including snacks)	Who gave and where	Events

MOTHERS: THIRD INTERVIEW

11 *Recent health, illness, events in household – and effects on child care as in 2.6 above.*

(a) Can I ask you how everyone in the household has been lately? Have you all been *well* (over last 4 weeks)?
For any household member's health problem

12 *Local preventive services – knowledge, acceptability, usefulness*

> *This section is intended to fill in our knowledge of parents' perspectives. It may be that we already have this knowledge from earlier interviews.*

Health visitor
Can I ask you about some of the health service staff?
You've told me about seeing the HV. Can I ask you:

(a) Do you think she's a good health visitor?
Prompts
What are the good things about her?
Any bad things?

(b) And what do you think is the health visitor's job? Anything else?

(c) Health visitors come to families with a baby or a small child and ask to come in and talk with you. Do you think that's all right?

Prompt
> Are you happy to have someone visiting you because you
> have a child/children?

(d) Were/was the health visitor/s useful to you when x was a baby
(under 6 months)?
In what ways?/for what?
Is she useful now? *Or, if says has no HV*: Are they useful now?
If yes, for what?
If no, Is that because you don't need help with x?
> Have you ever asked for help and not got it?

Clinic doctor/GP (Well-baby clinic)
(e) How about the doctor at the clinic, at the well-baby clinic?
Do you think s/he is good?
> *Prompts*
> What are the good things about her/him?
> Any bad things?

(f) What do you think is her/his job? Anything else?
> *Prompt*
> Are you happy with that?

(g) Have you found the doctor useful to you?
> *Prompts*
> When x was a baby? In what ways?
> And how about now?
> *If yes*: for what?
> *If no*: why is that?
Have you ever asked for help and not got it?

(h) Have you, as a parent, found the clinic useful? For what?
What are the good things about it? Any bad?
Research questions
(a) *What do parents think preventive service staff are aiming for?*
(b) *How acceptable is intervention?*
(c) *How useful are the services?*

13 *Child health care at home*

You've told me a lot about how you look after x, and the things you do for her. Could I go through some of the things you've talked about and ask you a bit more about them?

Could you tell me which are the most important things for keeping x healthy. *Get list.*

We've already talked about food. Can we go on to (e.g. exercise). Can you tell me:

For each topic ask:

Do you think that matters for her health?

What is it you are aiming to do/How will it help?

What happened about it yesterday/When was the most recent time that happened/you did that?

Do you find it easy to do that (e.g. give exercise)?. For instance what about yesterday/last time?

Are there any things that make it difficult? (e.g. housing, neighbourhood, money, transport, adults' work)?

Have you talked to anyone about it or read about it or asked for information or help?

(a) Some parents have told us about other kinds of care they think are important. Can I ask you what you think about them?

Cover:

mixing with other children

exercise

sleep

adults playing with children and talking with them

bowel movements/keeping children regular.

And for each ask:

Do you think that matters for health?

Do you do anything about that?

What about yesterday/when was the most recent time?

If it is seen as important: do you find it easy to do that?

Any problems yesterday/most recent time?

Are there any things that make it difficult including that? (e.g. housing, neighbourhood, transport, adults' work)?

Have you talked with anyone about that, or read about it or asked for information or help?

Research questions

(a) *What do parents perceive to be good forms of preventive health care?*

(b) *What are their constraints and opportunities for carrying them out?*

(c) *Do they turn for information or help to any source (media, lay, professional)?*

14 *Demographic data*

Can I ask you a few questions about you and the rest of the household?
Do you mind if I just go through these questions to make sure I've got it right?

(a) *Household*: There's X and Y and Z living here together. Is that right?
And anyone else living in the house or that you see every day usually?

(b) *Care of x*: And who looks after x during the day?
Care-giving arrangements in x's day, over the 7-day week.

(c) *Paid work*: And can I ask about paid work:
Do you do any?
  type of job
  hours worked per day
  no. of days worked
  (establish total no. of hours worked per week).
If not in paid work: What was your most recent job?
Establish:
  employed/self-employed
  manager/not manager
If not able to talk with father:
Can you tell me – does x's father (etc) do any paid work at present?
Establish:
  type of job
  hours worked per day
  no. of days worked (hours worked per week).
If not in paid work: What was his most recent job?
Establish:
  employed/self-employed

manager/not manager

(d) *Income*   Can I ask you to give me a rough idea of your household income? (We're trying to see whether parents have a reasonable income for looking after the family and the children.)
Could you look at this card (Table A1) and say which income bracket/range/set you are in as a household? After tax – net income (including benefits).

Table A1

	Weekly	Monthly
A	£0 – £5	£0 – £20
B	£6 – £15	£24 – £60
C	£16 – £25	£64 – £100
D	£26 – £35	£104 – £140
E	£36 – £45	£144 – £180
F	£46 – £55	£184 – £220
G	£56 – £65	£224 – £260
H	£66 – £85	£264 – £340
I	£86 – £105	£344 – £420
J	£106 – £125	£424 – £500
K	£126 – £145	£504 – £580
L	£146 – £165	£584 – £660
M	£165 – £200	£660 – £800
N	over £200	over £800

(e) And do you get any state benefits?
   If so, which?

Not receiving any benefits	.....	Free prescriptions	.....
Child benefit	.....	Free school meals	.....
One-parent benefit	.....	Housing benefit	.....
Family income supplement	.....	Other (please explain)	....
Supplementary allowance	......	....	
Free milk and vitamins	......	....	

(c) Do you have to pay for housing out of your net income?
(d) Do you feel you have enough to manage on?
   And to look after x as you want to?

(f) *Birth-place, mobility*
Can I ask you where you were *born?*
If abroad, How old were you when you came to the UK?
So how long have you lived in the UK?
How long have you lived in London:
   in this area?
   in this flat/house?
If *applicable*: So how many places have you lived since x was born?
Ask (e) for both parents.

(g) So you went to school in . . . country?
Which grade did you reach (e.g. for Indian sub-continent schools)?
Did you pass any exams?
Have you done any courses, training, qualified for any work since then?

(h) Can you tell me what is the language you speak at home, and with friends?
If English: do you speak any languages apart from English?
Do you feel you know English well enough to talk with the HV, the doctor, other people you *have* to deal with?

(i) Were you brought up in any religion/any faith?
Do you feel you have a religion/faith now?
Is it a help, for living round here/caring for x?

(j) *Housing*
Make sure you have established:
type of housing: flat, house, rooms
tenure: private, council, owned
floor: of entrance door
garden: yes, no, shared
crowding: no. of people for no. of rooms.

15. As in question 5.

INTERVIEW WITH FATHER OR OTHER CARE–GIVER

1   Now you have a child in the household, has it altered your way of life? First of all, in practical ways?

Prompt
Do you spend your time differently?

2 Do you feel differently as a person now you have/there is a child in the household?
Prompt
Do you enjoy being a parent?

3 How much time each day do you spend with x? Are you sometimes in charge (how many hours a day/week)?

4 What is it like looking after x/having x around now, compared to 6 months ago?
Prompt
Has she changed? What differences do you notice in her now?

5 (a) Can I ask you: what do you see as your role and responsibility as a parent?
Prompt
Are there some things *you* take responsibility for? What are they?

(b) If we take some (specific) things parents have to decide about, can I ask:
what about immunization – who decided what to do?
any recent changes in how your child is looked after, for instance the food she eats, when she sleeps, toilet-training, how she spends the day, who she spends the day with – who decided about these?

6 And if x shows signs of becoming ill:
Prompts
Who notices first?
Who looks after her?
Who decides what to do?
Who decides whether, or when to take her to a doctor/ask for help?
Can you tell me about the last time x was ill?
Prompts
Who noticed first?
Who looked after her?
Who decided what to do?
Who decided whether, or when to take her to a doctor/ask for help?

7 (a) Have you talked to any doctor or HV about x recently (in last 4 weeks)?

Can you tell me about that?
> *Prompt*
>> Were you happy with (this meeting)?
>> Did you have enough time to talk about it?
>> Did you feel s/he respected your views?

(b) Have you met your HV? Do you think she's good? Any bad things about her?

(c) What do you see as being her job? Anything else?

(d) Health visitors come to families with small children and ask to come in and talk with parents. Do you think that's alright?

8 Can I ask you a couple of questions about your own health *(GHS questions):*

(a) Over the last 12 months, would you say your health has on the whole been good, fairly good or not good?

(b) Do you have any long-standing illness, disability or infirmity? By long-standing, I mean anything that has troubled you over a period of time or that is likely to affect you over a period of time? *If so:*
> What is the matter with you?
> Does this illness or disability limit your activities in any way?

(c) Now I'd like you to think about the 2 weeks ending yesterday. During those 2 weeks did you have to cut down on any of the things you usually do (about the house, at work or in your free time) because of (answer to b or some other) illness or injury? *If so:*
> How many days was this in all, during those 2 weeks?

9 Having a child in the household, has it made any difference to how you look after your own health?
> *Prompt*
>> Are you concerned about your own health (more or less since x was born?
>> Do you usually/routinely do anything to keep yourself healthy?
>> What?
>> And has that changed since x was born? How and why?

10 (a) Can you describe a child in the best possible health?

(b) How do you think children get to that state of health/What do you think makes a child healthy like that?

(c) Do you feel able (you yourself or you the adults in the household) to give x all she needs to keep her in the best of

health? Why? Why not?
   (d) What part do you play in that?
11 Can I finally ask you about paid work. Do you do any paid work
    at present?
       If so:
          Can you tell me what your job is?
          Are you self-employed or employed by others?
          Are you a manager?
And:
   What are your hours of work?
   Per day and per week?
If not currently in paid work: Can you tell me what was your
most recent job?
       Prompts
          As above.
          Can you tell me what that was?
          Were you self-employed or employed by others?
          Were you a manager?
And:
   What were your hours of work?
   Per day and per week?
Research questions
(a) *What part do others in household (apart from mother or main
     care-giver) perceive they play in child-care?*
(b) *What part do others perceive they play specifically in health care
     of children?*
(c) *How do parents and other adults say they divide up responsibility
     for decision-making about the child's health and welfare?*
(d) *What difference to others' perspectives on use of time, own
     identity, and self-health care does arrival of a first child make?*

INTERVIEW WITH CLINICAL MEDICAL OFFICERS

1 (a) Could I start by asking you how you spend your working week?
  (b) If we take last week, can you tell me as regards under-5s:
       What did you most want to do? Did you manage it?
       What were the most satisfying parts of the working week?
       And the least satisfying?
       Would you say you had some/any successes?
       And any failures?

2   Can you tell me about the most recent session when you did an 18-month developmental check?
    Prompts
        What did you see as the purposes of the session?
        How did you see your role?
        Did you feel it was a success?
        What do you think the parent(s) got from it?
        In general, do you think it is an important service?
        And do you think parents value it?

3   Can you tell me about the most recent occasion when the topic of immunization came up with a parent?
        What did you see as the purposes of the session?
        How did you see your role?
        Did you feel it was a success?
        What do you think the parent(s) got from it?
        In general, do you think it is an important service?
        And do you think parents value it?

4 (a) How would you describe a really healthy child of 21 months?
  (b) What do you think brings about (such really) good health in a child?

5 (a) With a child of that age, are there some health care practices which you think are important for keeping the child healthy?
  (b) What factors make it easy for parents to do these things? And what makes it difficult?
  (c) Do you raise/discuss these topics with the parents? Why?

6 *Two child-rearing topics: food and social contacts*

Can we take a couple of specific topics to do with child-rearing (as regards children aged 21 months or so).

Food

(a) How important do you think food is? And why?

(b) What do you think are good practices on food for this age-group?

(c) Do some of the parents need help on nutrition for their children (i.e. according to doctor's criteria of good practices)?

(d) Do some of the parents have difficulties giving good care (according to doctor's criteria)? Why?

(e) Do you try to introduce this topic, routinely, for this age-group?

7 Contacts with other children

(a) How important do you think contact with other children is? And why?

(b) What do you think are good practices on contacts with other children for this age-group?

(c) Do some of the parents need help on contacts with other children (i.e. according to CMO's criteria on good practices)?

(d) Do some of the parents have difficulties (according to CMO's criteria)? Why?

(e) Do you try to introduce this topic, routinely, for this age-group?

8 Child welfare: three topics

Can I ask you your ideas on some specific points to do with children's welfare?

(a) Some children eat a lot of sweets and sugary things. How do you account for that?

(b) I expect you know that children in working class households (especially in class V) are more likely than other children to have *accidents.*

Why do you think that is?

(c) *Child abuse*

There's been a lot of talk recently about child abuse.

What do you think causes some parents to injure their children?

What do you see as your role with regard to child abuse?

9 (a) What do you see as the purposes functions? of the preventive child health services?

(b) Do you think they are well organized structured (staffed) to carry out these purposes/functions?

(c) How do you see the HV's role in the services?

10 (a) What do you see as your role within these services?

(b) Is it easy for you to do those things?

What are the difficulties?

(c) Do you feel you are successful in your job?

11 (a) What do parents need from the preventive child health services?

Prompt

Is that all parents?

(b) What do you think are their perceptions of the functions of the services and their value?

12 (a) Thinking about the population of the area you work in, do you think the preventive child health services are appropriate for serving the people?

(b) And are they successful?

(c) Are there ways in which they could be made more appropriate and successful?

(d) Do you think the services in this area have responded to the fact that we are now a multi-ethnic society?

13 *Background data*

Can I ask you a bit about your own background and career?

Could you tell me about your career to date, education and training including duration of each, jobs, including the present training for paediatric work, any in-service training (or training since initial training).

Do you have any children of your own?

Do you enjoy this work?

What are your career plans and aims?

Research questions

(a) *What do CMOs see as factors leading to optimal health in children?*

(b) *What do they think facilitates and constrains parents in their work of child health care (i.e. explanations for 'good' health care)?*

(c) *What do they see as the purpose of the preventive child health services?*

(d) *What do they see as parental needs from the preventive child health services?*

(e) *How appropriate and successful do they think the preventive child health services are in serving the local people?*

(f) What do they see as their role within those services? What is the appropriate division of labour between parents, health visitors, doctors?

APPENDIX 3
OTHER STUDIES TO WHICH WE MAKE FREQUENT REFERENCE

GRAHAM, H. AND MCKEE, L. (1979)

This study (1976–7) (carried out in a northern town in England) was concerned with women's experience of late pregnancy, childbirth and the first 6 months of motherhood. The study sample comprised 100 women expecting their first baby and 100 expecting their second. The 200 women were interviewed during the last 3 months of pregnancy at one month after the baby's birth and 4 months later. From this sample a smaller sample of 120 was drawn, and more detailed interviews carried out.

MOSS, P., BOLLAND, G., FOXMAN, R. AND OWEN, C. (1986)

This study (1979–81) aimed to explore the transition to parenthood. A sample was drawn from a district general hospital in the outer suburbs of London. The sample was stratified by class and included 90 families: half middle class and half working class. All parent pairs were aged 20–34, were married and were born in the UK or Eire; the mother had 'booked in' to the hospital before 20 weeks of pregnancy. Interviews were carried out with the mother twice in pregnancy and at 7 weeks, 6 months and 12 months after the child's birth. Fathers were interviewed three times: during the pregnancy, about 8 weeks after birth and at 12 months.

MCINTOSH, J. (1987)

This study (1981–4) focused on the transition to motherhood of working class mothers. A random sample of first-time mothers was drawn from three Glasgow ante-natal clinics. Eighty mothers were recruited and 60 remained in the study throughout the interview period. Six semi-structured interviews were carried out over the period: 7 months into pregnancy to 9 months after the child's birth. The study covered mother's experiences and attitudes to health services, including the health visitor.

GRAHAM, H. (1985 and 1987)

The study (1984) focused on the organization of health care in households and the organization of material resources for family health. A sample of 88 families with pre-school children were randomly chosen from a household survey in Milton Keynes, and 14 more were found using 'snowball' sampling (102 in all). Mothers were interviewed using a semi-structured schedule; they also filled in a health profile and (most) a 24-hour diary.

SEFI, S. (1988)

This exploratory study aimed to explore aspects of the relationship between mothers of first babies and health visitors. It focused on conversations during home visits and comprised tape-recordings of visits from five health visitors to nine first-time mothers from the 'new birth visit' to a visit when the child was 8 weeks old. The tape-recordings were analysed using conversation analysis methods.

REFERENCES AND FURTHER READING

Akinsanya J. A. (1988). Ethnic minority nurses, midwives and health visitors: what role for them in the National Health Service. *New Community*; **XIV**: no 3: 444–50.

Allsop J. (1986). Primary health care – the politics of change. *Journal of Social Policy*; 15: part 4, 489–96.

Armstrong D. (1983). *Political Anatomy of the Body: Medical Knowledge in Britain in the 20th Century*. Cambridge, Cambridge University Press.

Ayton M. (1987). *Bridging The Gap: Perspectives on Consumer Participation in the Health Visiting and School Nursing Service*. London: Health Visitors Association. (November 1987).

Baker J. (1986). Comparing national priorities: family and population policy in Britain and France. *Journal of Social Policy*; 15: 4: 421–42.

Balint M. (1964). *The Doctor, His Patient and the Illness*. London: Pitman Medical.

Barclay Report (1982). *Social Workers: Their Role and Tasks*. London. Bedford Square Press.

Black Report (1980). *Inequalities in Health: Report of a Research Working Group*. London: HMSO.

Boulton M. G. (1983). *On Being a Mother*. London: Tavistock Publications.

Brent Community Health Council (1981). *Black People and the Health Service*. April 1981.

British Association of Social Workers and Health Visitors Association (1982). *The Role of the Health Visitor in Child Abuse*. Joint Statement, December 1982.

Brook E., Davis A. (eds) (1985). *Women, The Family and Social Work*. London: Tavistock Publications.

Brown C. (1984). *Black and White Britain: The Third Policy Studies Institute Survey*. London: Heinemann Educational Books.

Brown J. (1988). *Child Benefit: Investing in the Future*. London: Child Poverty Action Group.

Campbell B. (1988). *Unofficial Secrets: Child Sexual Abuse: The Cleveland Case*. London: Virago.

Charles N., Kerr M. (1986). Issues of responsibility and control in the feeding of families. In *The Politics of Health Education: Raising the Issues*, Rodmell S., Watt A. eds. pp. 57–75. London: Routledge and Kegan Paul.

Cohen B. (1988). *Caring for Children: Services and Policies for Childcare and Equal Opportunities in the United Kingdom*. Report for the European Commission's Childcare Network. Commission of the European Communities, 8 Storey's Gate, London SW1 3AT.

Crawford R. (1977). You are dangerous to your health: the ideology and politics of victim blaming. *International Journal of Health Services*; 7: no. 4.

Cresson, G. (1986). Une femme à son chevet. *Sociales Informations – Famille et Santé*: no. 4, 66–72.

Currer C. (1983). *The Mental Health of Pathan Mothers in Bradford: A Case Study of Migrant Asian Women* (Final Report). University of Warwick.

Dally A. (1982). *Inventing Motherhood: The Consequences of an Ideal*. London: Burnett.

David M. (1985). Motherhood and social policy – a matter of education? *Critical Social Policy*; 12: 28–43.

Department of Health and Social Security (1976). *Prevention and Health: A Reassessment of Public and Personal Health*. London: HMSO.

Department of Health and Social Security (1986a). *Primary Health Care: An Agenda for Discussion*. Cmnd 9771, London: HMSO.

Department of Health and Social Services (1986b). *Neighbourhood Nursing: A Focus for Care* (The Cumberlege Report). London: HMSO.

Dingwall R. (1977). *The Social Organisation of Health Visitor Training*. London: Croom Helm.

Dingwall R. (1982). Community nursing and civil liberties. *Journal of Advanced Nursing*; 7: 337–46.

Dingwall R., Eekelaar J., Murray T. (1983). *The Protection of Children: State Intervention and Family Life*. Oxford: Blackwell.

Dingwall R., Rafferty A-M., Webster C (1988). *An Introduction to the Social History of Nursing*. London: Routledge and Kegan Paul.

Donovan J. (1986). *We Don't Buy Sickness, It Just Comes*. London: Gower Publications.

Draper J., Farmer S., Field S., Thomas H. (1983). *The Early Parenthood Project: A Study of Health Visiting Practice in the Cambridge Health District* (1982–83). Cambridge: Hughes Hall.

Draper P., Griffiths J., Dennis J., Popay J. (1980). Three types of health education. *British Medical Journal*; 281: 493–95.

Drennan V. (1986). *Working In A Different Way*. Paddington and North Kensington Health Authority.

Drennan V (ed.) (1988). *Health Visitors and Groups: Politics and Practice*. Oxford: Heinemann Medical Books.

Dyson S. (1986). Professional services: the main problem facing parents of mentally handicapped children. *Radical Health Promotion*, no. 4, Summer/Autumn 1986.

Elbourne D., Richardson M., Chalmers I., Waterhouse I., Holt E (1987). The Newbury maternity care study: a randomised controlled trial to assess a policy of women holding their own obstetric records. *British Journal of Obstetrics and Gynaecology*; **94**: 612–19.

Farrant W., Russell J. (1986). *The Politics of Health Information*. Bedford Way Paper No. 25. London: University of London Institute of Education.

Fawcett-Hennessy A. (1986). Who is the key worker? *Community Care*; 3rd April 1983: 20–21.

French J., Adams L. (1986). From analysis to synthesis: theories of health education. *Health Education Journal*; **45**: 71–4.

Freire P. (1972). *Pedagogy of the Oppressed*. Harmondsworth, Middx: Penguin.

Foster M-C. (1988a). The French puéricultrice. *Children and Society*, **2**: 4.

Foster M-C. (1988b). Multi-ethnic health in Paris. *Health Services Journal* 15th December 1988.

Freeman S (1983). Psychological insights. In *Health Visiting* (Owen G. ed.) London: Baillière Tindall.

General Household Survey 1985 (1987). London: HMSO.

Graham H. (1979a). Women's attitudes to the child health services. *Health Visitor Journal*; **52**: 175–78.

Graham H. (1979b). Prevention and health: every mother's business. A comment on child health policies in the 1970s. In *The Sociology of the Family* (Harris C., ed.) University of Keele: Sociological Monograph no. 25.

Graham H. (1984). *Women, Health and the Family*. Brighton: Wheatsheaf Books.

Graham H. (1985). *Caring for the family. Report to the Health Education Council*. London: Health Education Council.

Graham H. (1987). Women's Smoking and Family Health. *Social Science and Medicine*; **25**, no. 1: 47–56.

Graham H., McKee L. (1979). *The first months of motherhood. Report of a survey of women's experiences of pregnancy, childbirth and the first six months after birth*. London: Health Education Council.

Graham H., Oakley A. (1986). Competing ideologies of reproduction: medical and maternal perspectives on pregnancy. In *Concepts of Health Illness and Disease* (Currer C., Stacey M., eds.) Leamington Spa: Berg.

Greene A., MacFarlane A. (1985). Parent-held child health record cards – a comparison of types. *Health Visitor Journal*, 58, no. 1: 14–15.

Griffiths Report (1983). *NHS Management Enquiry*. DA(83)38. London: HMSO.

Hall D. M. B. (ed.) (1989). *Health for All Children: a Programme for Child Health Surveillance*. Oxford: Oxford Medical Publications, OUP.

Hardyment C. (1984). *Dream Babies: Child Care From Locke to Spock* Oxford: Oxford University Press.

Harrison J. (1986). *The Workloads of Health Visitors in Sheffield*. Sheffield Health Authority.

Health Visitors Association (1987a). *Health Visiting and School Nursing Reviewed*. London: Health Visitors Association.

Health Visitors Association (1987b). *Aspects of Child Abuse*. London: Health Visitors Association.

Health Visitors Association (in press). *Guidance for Members on Professional Practice in Multicultural/multiracial Britain*.

Helman C. (1984). *Culture, Health and Illness*. Bristol: John Wright and Sons Ltd.

Hewitt M. (1958). *Wives and Mothers in Victorian Industry*. London: Rockcliff.

HMSO (1987). *Promoting Better Health: The Government's Programme for Improving Primary Health Care*. Cmnd 249. London: HMSO.

Hoyles M. (ed.) (1980). *Changing Childhood*. London: Writers and Readers Publishing Cooperative.

Hughes M., Mayall B., Moss P., Perry J., Petrie P., Pinkerton G. (1980). *Nurseries Now*. Harmondsworth, Middx: Penguin.

Husband C. (ed.) (1982). *Race in Britain: Continuity and Change*. London: Hutchinson and Co. Ltd.

Jefferys M., Sachs H. (1983). *Rethinking General Practice: Dilemmas in Primary Medical Care*. London: Tavistock Publications.

Jordan B., Parton N. (1983). *The Political Dimensions of Social Work*. Oxford: Basil Blackwell.

Joshi H. (1987). The cost of caring. In *Women and Poverty in Britain* (Glendinning C., Millar J., eds.) Brighton: Wheatsheaf Books.

Kamerman S., Kahn A. (1980). *Child care, family benefits and working parents. A study in Comparative Policy*. (Cross national studies – A Research Report). New York: Columbia University, School of Social Work.

Laing R. (1986). The health visitor's role in child abuse. *Child Abuse Review*; 1: 10–13.

Land H. (1978). Who cares for the family? *Journal of Social Policy*; 7 no. 3.

Land H. (1983). Who still cares for the family – recent developments in income maintenance, taxation and family law. In *Women's Welfare, Women's Rights* (Lewis J., ed.) London: Croom Helm.

Lewis C. (1986). *Becoming A Father*. Milton Keynes: Open University Press.

Lewis C., O'Brien M. (1987). *Reassessing Fatherhood: New Observations on Fathers and the Modern Family*. London: Sage Publications.

Lewis J. (1980). *The Politics of Motherhood. Child and Maternal Welfare in England 1900–1939*. London: Croom Helm.

Marsh P. (1987). Social work and fathers – an exclusive practice. In *Reassessing Fatherhood: New Observations on Fathers and the Modern Family* (Lewis C., O'Brien M., eds.) London: Sage Publications.

Mayall B. (1986). *Keeping Children Healthy*. London: Allen and Unwin.

Mayall B., Grossmith C. (1984). *Caring for the Health of Young Children*.

Report to the Economic and Social Research Council, August 1984. London: Economic and Social Research Council.

Mayall B. (in press). The division of labour in child health care. *Journal of Social Policy*.

McClymont A. (1980). *Teaching For Reality*. London: Council for the Education and Training of Health Visitors.

McIntosh J. (1987) *A Consumer Perspective on the Health Visiting Service*. University of Glasgow, Social Pediatric and Obstetric Research Unit.

Mintern L., Lambert W. L. (1984). *Mothers of Six Cultures: Antecedents of Child Rearing*. New York: Wiley.

Moss P. (1986). *Child Care in the Early Months: How Child Care Arrangements are Made for Babies*. Thomas Coram Research Unit Working and Occasional Paper No. 3. Thomas Coram Research Unit, 41 Brunswick Square, London WC1N 1AZ.

Moss P., Bolland G., Foxman R., Owen C. (1986). The first six months after birth: mothers' views of health visitors. *Health Visitor Journal*; 59: 71–74.

Naidoo J. (1986). Limits to individualism. In *The Politics of Health Education* Rodmell, S. and Watt, A. (eds.) pp. 17–37. London: Routledge and Kegan Paul.

National Children's Bureau (1987). *Investing in the Future: Child Health Ten Years After the Court Report*. A Report of the Policy and Practice Review Group. London: National Children's Bureau.

Nicoll A. (1983). Community child health services – for better or worse? *Health Visitor Journal*; 56: 241–43.

Oakley A. (1981). Normal motherhood: an exercise in self-control. In *Controlling Women: The Normal and the Deviant* (Hutter B., Williams G., eds.). London: Croom Helm.

Oakley A. (1986). On the importance of being a nurse. In *Telling the Truth About Jerusalem* (Oakley A., ed.) Oxford: Blackwells.

Orr J. (1986). Feminism and health visiting. In *Feminist Practice in Women's Health Care* (Webb C., ed.) Chichester: John Wiley and Sons.

Ottey T. Quoted in Mares P., Henley A., Baxter C. (1985). *Health Care in Multiracial Britain*. London: Health Education Council, National Extension College Trust Ltd.

Pearson M. (1986). Racist notions of ethnicity and culture in health education. In *The Politics of Health Education: Raising the Issues*. (Rodmell S. and Watt A., eds.) pp. 38–56. London: Routledge and Kegan Paul.

Popay J., Dhooge Y., Shipman C. (1986). *Unemployment and Health: What Role for Health and Social Services?* London: Health Education Council Research Report no. 3.

Prout A. (1986). *An Analytical Ethnography of Sickness Absence in an English Primary School*. PhD Thesis, Department of Social Anthropology, University of Keele.

Phoenix A. (1989). Black women and the maternity services. In *The Politics of Maternity Care* (Garcia J., Kilpatrick R., Richards M. (eds.)). Oxford: Oxford University Press.

Richards M. (1980). *Infancy: World of the Newborn*. London: Harper Row.

Richman N. (1974). The effects of housing on pre-school children and their mothers. *Developmental Medicine and Child Neurology*; **16**: 53–8.

Richman N. (1976). Depression in mothers of young children. *Journal of Child Psychology and Psychiatry*; **17**: 75–78.

Riley D. (1983). *War in the Nursery*. London: Virago.

Robinson J. (1982). *An Evaluation of Health Visiting*. London: Council for the Education and Training of Health Visitors.

Royal College of General Practitioners (1982). *Healthier Children – Thinking Prevention*. London: Royal College of General Practitioners.

Runnymede Trust of Radical Statistics Group (1980). *Britain's Black Population*. London: Heinemann Educational Books.

Russell G. (1983). *The Changing Role of Fathers*. Milton Keynes: The Open University Press.

Rutter M., Madge N. (1976). *Cycles of Deprivation*. London: Heinemann.

Sachs H. (1988). A theoretical framework for health visiting. In *Health Visiting – Theory and Practice* Report of a Day Conference held at the Thomas Coram Research Unit (Mayall, B., Foster, M-C, eds.). Thomas Coram Research Unit, 41 Brunswick Square, London WC1N 1AZ.

Saffin K. (1985). French lessons *Community Outlook – Nursing Times*; **81**: 24–6.

Salvage J. (1985). *The Politics of Nursing*. London: Heinemann Medical Books.

Scarr S., Dunn J. (1987). *Mother Care/Other Care*. Harmondsworth, Middx: Penguin.

Sefi S. (1988). Health visitors talking to mothers. *Health Visitors Journal*; **61**: 7–10.

Sefi S., Macfarlane A. (1985). Child health clinics: why mothers attend. *Health Visitor Journal*; **58**: 129–30.

Stacey M. (1976). The health service consumer: a sociological misconception. In *The Sociology of the National Health Service* (Stacey M., ed.). *Sociological Review Monograph*, **22**. University of Keele.

Stacey M. (1988). *The Sociology of Health and Healing: A Textbook*. London: Unwin Hyman.

Stacey M., Davies C. (1983). *Division of Labour in Child Health Care*. Final Report to the Social Science Research Council. University of Warwick.

Steedman C. (1982). *The Tidy House*. London: Virago.

Strehlow M. (1983). *Education for Health*, London: Harper Row.

Strong P. M. (1979). Sociological imperialism and the profession of medicine. *Social Science and Medicine*; **13A**: 199–215.

Strong P., Robinson J. (1988). *New Model Management: Griffiths and the NHS*. University of Warwick: Nursing Policy Studies Centre.

Tizard B., Hughes M. (1984). *Young Children Learning*. London: Fontana.

Tizard J., Moss P., Perry J. (1976). *All Our Children*. London: Temple Smith.

Townsend P., Davidson N. (1982). *Inequalities in Health* (The Black Report). Harmondsworth, Middx: Penguin.

Walker A., Walker C. (1987). *The Growing Divide: A Social Audit* 1979–1987. Child Poverty Action Group, 1–5 Bath Street, London EC1V 9PY.

Wallman S. (1984). Eight London Households. London: Tavistock Publications.

Webster C. (1988). *The Health Services Since the War* vol. I *Problems of Health Care*. London: HMSO.

Welburn V. (1980). *Post-Natal Depression*. London: Macmillan.

Wilson E. (1977). *Women and the Welfare State*. London: Tavistock.

Wilson G. (1987). Money: patterns of responsibility and irresponsibility in marriage. In *Give and Take in Families: Studies in Resource Distribution* (Brannen J., Wilson G., eds.) London: Allen and Unwin.

Winnicott D. W. (1964). *The Child, The Family and the Outside World*. Harmondsworth, Middx: Penguin.

Wohl A. S. (1983). *Endangered Lives: Public Health in Victorian Britain*. London: Dent and Sons.

World Health Organisation (1985). *Working Group on Today's Health – Tomorrow's Wealth: New Perspectives in Prevention in Childhood*. Summary Report of meeting at Kiev, 21–25 October 1985. ICP/MCH 102/m 04(S). Geneva: WHO Regional Office for Europe.

World Health Organisation (1986). A discussion document on the concept and principles of health promotion. In *Health Promotion*: **1**, no. 1; 73–6, May 1986.

Wright-Mills C. (1970). *The Sociological Imagination*. Harmondsworth, Middx: Penguin.

INDEX